# The Last Law Giver

*In the name of Allah, the Beneficent and the*

*Merciful—*

# The Last Law Giver

### (with Biblical quotations)

By

## MAHMOOD VANDERMAN

### Author of

*" HOW TO PRAY ", ' TEACHINGS OF ISLAM ", Etc*

### with a Foreword

By

### The Hon'ble Nawab Mahdi Yar Jung Bahadur,
### Political & Educational Member,
### H. E. H. The Nizam's Govt.,
### Hyderabad-Dn.

# DEDICATED

*with affectionate and grateful regard*

TO

## THE HON'BLE SIR AKBAR HYDARI, Kt., B.A, LL. D.
## NAWAB HYDER NAWAZ JUNG BAHADUR

IN

Profound admiration of his meritorious and noble services in all spheres of nation-building activities to the Premier Indian State and its people under the patronage of its August and Most Enlightened Ruler, of which the financing of various huge Irrigation Projects, the founding of Osmania University and the revival of Ancient Archaeological Monuments, ruins and archives are the special landmarks.

And above all

Whose every day life is inspired by the behests laid down by the Prophet and who is a true devotee of the principles of Islam of the Universal brotherhood. and ceaselessly trying to promote mutual good relations and love between the different communities of India.

——0——

# FOREWORD.

----

Mr. Mahmood Vanderman is a Muslim by faith and by conviction, and a very sincere one too. I have rarely seen among those who are converts to the faith any person who is so zealous in its cause.

The present book that Mr. Vanderman has compiled about the Holy Prophet of Islam is the outcome of his love and reverence for the Prophet and does not fail to inspire the reader with a similar feeling. In it are collected together many extracts from the writings of men of various nations—European as well as Indian—who though not Muslims themselves, have felt constrained to pay the highest tribute to the Prophet's work and teachings and to acknowledge the greatness of Islam both as a religion and as a practical rule of life.

Mr. Vanderman intends to publish translations of this work in the local vernaculars—Telugu, Kanarese and Marati. I consider that this is a very good idea as it will help to spread a correct knowledge of Islam and dispel any false notions or prejudices that may still exist in the minds of men who have not given sufficient thought to the subject.

I wish him every success in this enterprise.

Hyderabad-Dn.
14th August 1935

MAHDI YAR JUNG.

# PREFACE

Of the many life-stories of the world's eminent personalities, that of the Holy Prophet Muhammad being most exhortative and adaptable at all times to all nations, I was revolving since a long time, the idea of producing a vivid picture of the Prophet, in English and the three other popular vernaculars— Telugu, Kanarese and Marati. My heart leaps with unbounded joy as my dream has at last taken a material shape in the form of the present work. In spite of the voluminous out-pour of Quranic literature, a major portion of the world is still in dark about the life and teachings of the Holy Prophet of Islam and to that section I extend this book which, I hope, will be instrumental in dispelling all mis-understanding about Islam and insinuating a thirst to know more about its principles and founder. The sole panacea of all communal antagonisms is a proper understanding of the various religions, and Dr. Paranjyapi, the Vice-Chancellor of Lucknow University in his Poona speech has rightly said, "When we know each other's religions thoroughly well, we will try to respect their sentiments and avoid the communal tension and troubles." If this is fulfilled my aim is attained.

I am greatly indebted to Nawab Lutuf-ud-Dowlah Bahadu· Sir Akbar Hydari, Nawab Rafat ii

Yar Jung Bahadur, Nawab Mehdi Yar Jung Baha-
dur, Nawab Fakher Yar Jung Bahadur, Nawab
Muzaffer Nawaz Jung Bahadur, Nawab Akhther Yar
Jung Bahadur, Nawab Dost Muhammad Khan,
Mr. Fazal Muhammad Khan and Mr. Liakatullah
Khan for the material and moral support they have
given me in bringing out this book to a success.

Further, I have to thank Prof. Abdul Khader
Saheb of the Osmania University for his valuable
suggestions on matters theological, to Mr. C. I.
Andrews, Journalist. for helping me in correcting
proofs and rendering literary co-operation, and
to Mr. K. S. Rajgopal, Proprietor of Osmania
General Agency for supplying paper in right
time and his keen interest to bring out the book
from Press at an early date.

While the book is being placed in the hands of
the public, I earnestly pray to the all-knowing
Allah to pour forth his choicest blessings and boun-
tiful mercy on all those who read it. May He aid
them to realise fraternity, liberty and equality in
their truest sense in accordance with the dictates of
the Last Law Giver.

May it be for the Glory of God.

1st October 1935.                    M. VANDERMAN.

Hyderabad-Dn.

# CONTENTS.

———

                                                               Page.

## Chapter I.

The unrivalled Prophetic mission  ..          ...1

## Chapter II.

Some of the distinctive points of superiority of
the Holy Prophet of Islam over all other
Prophets          ...          ..          ... 55

## Chapter III.

Muhammed According to the Holy Quran    ... 60

## Chapter IV.

*What others say about the Last Law Giver:—*

1  Nepolean Bonaparte          ...          ... 67
2  George Bernard Shaw          ...          ... 67
3  Mahatma Gandhi ...          ...          ... 68
4  His Excellency Maharaja Sir Kishen Per-
   shad ...          ..          ..          ... 69
5  The Great Baba Nanak (founder of Sikh
   Religion)          ...          ...          ... 70
6  Sadhu T. L. Vaswani          ..          ... 72
7  Mrs. Sarojini Naidu          ...          ... 74
8  Mr. Lala Lajpat Rai          ...          ... 74
9  Major Arthur Glyn Leonard  ...          ... 74
10 Rev. Bossworth Smith          ...          ... 81
11 Rev. John Devenport          ...          ... 85

12  Sir Thomas Carlyle ..        ...        ..    93
13  Sir William Muir  ...        ...        ...   95
14  Rt. Rev. Bishop Richard Pococke        ...   98
15  Prof. T. W. Arnold  .        ..        .. 102
16  Prof. E. Monet of France        ..        .. 104
17  Stanley Lanepole  ..        ..        ... 105
18  Dr. Julius Germanus of Hungary        .. 106
19  Major General Forlong        . .        . 108
20  Dinet & Saliman  . .        . .        .. 110
21  Alfred Martin        . .        . .        ... 111
22  Prof. Ram Dev, (*Editor, Vedic Magazine, Lahore*)        ...        .        ... 112
23  The Editor, Sat Updesh, Lahore        ..  112
24  Dr. Gokalchand Ph.D., Bar-at-Law, Lahore  113
25  Dr. Marcus Dodds  ...        ...        ... 113
26  Rev. Stephens        .        ...        ... 115
27  Chamber's Cyclopaedia Vol. VI        . 118
28  Herbert lectures  ...        ...        .. 118
29  Edward Arnold  ...        ...        .. 119
30  Ameena Agnes Deaves        ...        ... 119
31  M. S Baboona  ...        ...        ... 119
32  A. J. Micheal  ...        ...        ... 119
33  J. A. Spronle  ...        ..        ... 120
34  Pierre Crabites  ...        ...        ... 120
35  Rev. Murray T. Titus        ...        ... 120
36  The Popular Encyclopaedia— ...        ... 121
           Division VII Page 326
37  Dean Stanely (Eastern Church)        ... 121
38  W. Irving        ... 121

39   Rev. Prof. Robertson          ...          ... 121
40   Encyclopaedia of Britanica    ...          ... 122
                    Vol. XVI Page 599
41   Rev. G. Margoliouth           ...          ... 122
42   Mungo Park       ...          ...          ... 123
43   Rev. Edward Blyden            ...          ... 123
44   Lawton ...        ...          ...          ... 124
45   Miss H. M. Lee    ...          ...          ... 125
46   Sir Charles Edward Archibald Hamilton ... 125
47   Rev. L. O'Leary, D.D.         ...          ... 126
48   Gibbon   ...          ...          ...          ... 126
49   Dr. Khalid Banning            ...          ... 126
50   Dr. A. Crichton, LL. D.       ...          ... 127

### Chapter V.

The Institution of Haj or Pilgrimage          ... 128

### Chapter VI.

The Ordinance of Ramzan or Fasting            ... 139

### Chapter VII.

Miraj or the Ascension of Prophet...          ... 147

### Chapter VIII.

What is Islam?        ...          ...          ... 155

# CHAPTER I.

## The Unrivalled Prophetic Mission.

Corruption has appeared in the land and the sea on account of what the hands of men have wrought.—HOLY QUR-AN, XXX 41.

Know that Allah gives life to the earth after its death.—LVI. 17.

IN these verses the God's inspired Book speaks of the corruption that prevailed in all countries of the world before the advent of the Holy child of this story. Death—mental, moral and spiritual death—had overtaken the human race and darkness prevailed everywhere clouding the beliefs and perverting the actions of the people. Judaism, Hinduism, Buddhism and other religions of the world, had lost all healthy influence on the lives of their followers. "The above religions have been reverted to heathenism, and the religious conception of the masses was only an infiltration of the Pagan cult. Besides, the souls of the dead were worshipped and their relics and images were the objects of chief adoration.

" The Christians of the seventh century had insensibly relapsed into a semblance of paganism , their public and private vows were addressed to the relics and images that disgraced the temples of the East  the throne of the Almighty was darkened by a crowd of martyrs, saints and angels, the objects of popular venaration, and the Collyridian heretics, who flourished in the fruitful soil of Arabia, invested the Virgin Mary with the name and honoures of a goddess The mysteries of the trinity and incarnation appear to contradict the principle of the Divine Unity. In their obvious sense, they introduce three equal deities, and transform the man Jesus into the substance of the son of God, an orthodox commentary will satisfy only a believing mind. The creed of Muhammad is free from the suspicion of ambiguity, and the Koran is a glorious testimony to the Unity of God "—GIBBON.

The social and moral condition of the world was equally deplorable. The followers of these religions had not only ceased to practise virtue, but vice itself had come to be looked upon as virtue, and men committed deadly sin to earn merit in the eye of the Lord. Every nation had sunk to a state of complete moral depravity. The corruption had appeared in the continents and on the islands. The statement may startle many, but it is the truth. The reader has but to remember that that time was the darkest period of the Middle Ages in Europe, and of the Mazdeic and Puranic ages in Persia and India respectively. Illicit sexual intercourse—a crime next only to murder in its consequences—was committed in the performance of various sacred rites. It was practised as a virtue with the sanction of religion. In the confessional in Christendom, more sin was committed than was washed away. "The condition of Constantinople under Justinian, the Christian and the glorified legislater, is the best

index to the demoralized and degraded state of society
all over Christendom. Public or private virtue had
no recognition in the social conceptions; a harlot
sat on the throne of the Cæsars, and shared with
the emperor the honours of the State. Theo-
dora had publicly plied her trade in the city
of Constantine. and her name was a byword
among its dissolute inhabitants. And now
she was adored as a queen in the same city by
'grave magistrates, orthodox bishops, victorious
generals, and captive monarchs.' The empire was
disgraced by her cruelties, which recognized no religious or moral restraint. Seditions, outbreaks,
and sanguinary tumults, in which the priesthood
always took the most prominent part, were the
order of the day. On these occasions every law,
human or divine, was trampled under foot, churches
and altars were polluted by atrocious murders; no
place was safe or sacred from depredations."[1] In
Persia, the Phallic cult, introduced centuries before
by Artaxerxes Mnemon, the brother of Cyprus, was
brought to its climax at that time by Mazdak who,
among his other abominable tenets, taught partner-
ship in women. He sanctified scenes of obscenity
accompanied by every kind of bacchanalian orgy.
This frightful communism in women was also
practised in India, under the teachings of
*Shaktakmat*, than in its prime in India. A *shaktak*

---

1 Syed Ameer Ali, *Spirit of Islam.*

priest could, of right, command the company of others' wives for his pleasure. Such demands were willingly obeyed, and the brides usually passed the first week of their honeymoon in the company of the high-priests. It was an act of virtue, and earned in their sight divine grace enough to bless their wedded life. The night of Shivratri, a Hindu festival, occasioned, in its celebration, an exhibition of the worst type of brutality when, under the influence of women and wine, even incestuous connections failed to excite any horror, since, indeed, the *Shaktak mantras* ( sacred hymns ) chanted on the occasion, ennobled everything foul and mean.

When such confusion and conglomeration was rampant about 13½ centuries ago, on 20.h April, 571 A. D. to be exact, a child was born in Mecca, a town of Arabia, situated about forty miles inland from the shores of the Red Sea. A child, one of the thousands that are born into the world everyday, but for whom the future held many surprising and wonderful things in store. The birth of the child gave rise to conflicting emotions in the hearts of his near ones, emotions both of joy and sorrow. There was joy because there was born to them a child who would continue the line of his forefathers and keep their name alive in the world. There was sorrow because the child reminded his

mother of her loving and most beloved husband
and his grandfather of a most obedient son, who
had left the world before the birth of his child.
His feature, his winning smile, the look of wonder
in his eyes with which he beheld this strange world
into which he had been so recently ushered; in
short, everything connected with him brought back
to the bereaved wife and the desolate father the
dear memories of the young husband and son who
had seven months previously left his dear ones to
return to His Maker. Joy, however, predominated
over sorrow, for the birth of this child was a guarantee that the name of the deceased would be
rescued from oblivion.

### THE ORIGIN OF ARABS.

The Arabs classify their fore fathers into three
clans:—

(a) Arab-i-Ariba, the original inhabitants of
the peninsula, who became extinct long before the
advent of the child referred above, but the ruins of
whose buildings can be seen to this day.

(b) Arab-i-Mutariba, those who followed the
oborigines and were made Arabs. They now
inhabit the outlying portions of Arabia, especially
Yemen.

(c) Arab-i-Mustariba, viz. those who became
Arabs by assimilation. These are the descendants

of Ishmæl, son of Abraham (on both of whom be
peace). They established themselves in the desert
of Hejaz. Amongst these is the family of Koresh,
to which the child narrated above belongs, and his
genealogy is traced back to Adnan, who lived 130
years before Jesus (on whom be peace). Adnan is,
by common consent, admitted to be a descendant of
Ishmæl.

About the year A. C. 200 a descendant of
Adnan named Fihr, surnamed Al-Koresh, acquired
great influence amongst his tribesmen ; and his descendant Kossay built a town round the Kaaba and
fixed the seat of Council (called Nadwa) at a house
(called Darunnadwa), where the Hanafi Mussala is
now situated, about 25 or 30 yards from the wall of
the Kaaba.

## THE FOUNDER OF THE CITY OF MECCA

Kossay seems to have been a man of very great
authority. He imposed a tax called the Rifada,
for the feeding of the poor pilgrims during their
three days' stay at Mina. He controlled the
administration of the wells of Mecca (Sikaya) and
had the custody of the keys of the Kaaba (Hijaba).
"He was king, magistrate, and chief pontiff," says
late Hon'ble Sir Syed Ameer Ali. He died in
A. C. 480. Under Kossay's administration the
Koresh acquired great wealth by means of trade
with Yemen, Syria, Mesopotamia, and Egypt.

Kossay had four sons, the fourth named Abd Menaf, from whom the hero of this narration is descended. Abd Menaf had four sons, of whom Hashim was the richest. Sheiba succeeded Hashim and was also called Muttalib. He had no sons, but vowed that if he had ten sons he would sacrifice one at the Kaaba. He had twelve sons and six daughters. The lot of being sacrificed fell on Abdullah, but this was redeemed by the payment of one hundred camels, which has since been fixed as the price of human blood.

## THE BIRTH AND YOUTH OF THE HOLY CHILD

Abdullah son of Abdul Mutalib was married to Amina, and the following year is the most famous year in the history of Arabia and of the World. It is the year of the invasion of Mecca by Abraha, the Abyssinian Viceroy of Yemen, accompanied by his elephants, hence called the year of the Elephant. Abraha as punished by God, and he and his army perished most miserably. Shortly after this event, Abdullah, on his journey to Yethreb (now called Medina), died in the twenty fifth year of his life and some days later the Holy child was born, on Monday, 12th of Rabial Awal (the year of the Elephant), and fifty days after the destruction of Abraha's army. His grandfather Abdul Mutalib

gave to this child who was born an orphan the
name of Muhammad and he began to thrive under
the care of his mother and of a wet nurse emplo-
ed by his uncle Abu Talib and was reared in the
desert for the first few years of his life. It was a
custom with the people of Mecca to entrust the care
and wet nursing of their children to the women in
the country, so that they might have the benefit
of the fresh air of the country, and should escape
the ill-effects of the confined air of the town.
Women belonging to villages 30 or 40 miles of
Mecca used to come to the town from time to time
and take away newly born babies for nursing, and
when they brought them back, after the period of
nursing was over, they used to be adequately rewarded for their care of the children by the parents
of the latter. When these women came to Mecca
after the birth of Muhammad his mother was also
anxious to entrust his care to some country woman,
but when a woman was told that the child was an
orphan she would refuse to under-take his nursing,
being apprehensive that the child's father being
dead, she would not be adequately rewarded for
her care of the child. This orphan child, who was
destined to be the Master of Kings and Emperors,
was Presented to each woman in turn and was by
each rejected. Strange, indeed, are the ways of
Providence. He had already provided means for
comforting the heart of this blessed child's mother,

and for his up-bringing in the country. Among those who had come to the town on this occasion to take in children for nursing, was one Haleema of Bani Saad who was a poor woman. As Muhammad, the blessed one, was presented to each woman and was rejected by all, so this woman went from house to house seeking a baby to nurse, but was sent away disappointed, as she was poor and nobody wished to entrust the care of their children to poor people. Having been rejected at every door, she made up her mind to take away this fatherless child, in order to avoid the taunts of her companions. When Muhammad had passed the period of nursing, Haleema brought him back to his mother, who took him to her parents at Madina. After a short stay at Madina, she was returning with the child to Mecca, when death overtook her, and at the age of six Muhammad was thus deprived of the loving care of his mother. Somebody conveyed him to his grandfather at Mecca. His grandfather, Abdul Muttalib, looked after him, but three years later he also joined his ancestors, and thus was the boy who was to rule the hearts of men for ever, the light of God, the prayer of Abraham left to himself. He had neither father, mother, brother, nor sister. In fact, except for a very brief period of his mother's company he had not known any of these relationships. His father had died before his birth, he never had any brothers or sisters. The homes in which his child-

hood was spent were neither wealthy nor cultivated.
For instance, meals were not served in those homes
in an orderly and regulated manner. The financial
condition and social habits of the people did not
encourage the observance of modern table manners.
At the time of the meals the children gathered
round the mother and clamoured for food, and each
made an attempt to appropriate to him or herself a
larger share than the others were able to secure.
Abu Talib's maid however, relates that Muhammad
never followed this habit. While the other
children were engaged in their unseemly contest
over the food, he would sit silently apart, wait-
ing for his aunt to give him his food, and whatever
he was given he ate with pleasure. The light of
God was shining all alone on the desert hills of
Arabia. But God was everything to him. His
communications and conversations were not so
much with men as with the whole host of universe:
the sun, the moon, and the stars up above ; the birds,
beasts, rain, clouds, and trees down below. He was
learning his lessons in the great school of Nature,
like the bee, "gathering honey all the day from
every opening flower." His was the spiritual honey.
In his twelfth year he followed his uncle Abu Talib
to Syria and was recognized by a saint called
Bahira, or Georges, or Sergius, as the coming
prophet and the most shining star of them all. In
his fourteenth year he was present at a war against

Benou Hawazin, but did not take any active part.
He spent his life in meditation and exaltation of
character and so great was the lustre he threw
around himself that he was unanimously named
Al-Amin, the Loyal, the Trustworthy, the Faithful.
No one before him had borne the name of Muhammad,
which means "the praised one" in Arabia; and no
one had been called Al-Amin. Thus did the voice
of humanity consciously and unconsciously recognized the pole-star of the world of spirituality.

## HIS HUMANITY.

At the age of twenty he joined the Society
whose members were required to take a vow that
they would, whenever called upon, help those who
were oppressed, whatever tribe they might belong
to, and secure to them the enjoyment of their proper
rights. So that, even in his early youth, when he
learnt that one man was being oppressed by another,
he would espouse the cause of the former and was
not satisfied until he had secured for him his just
right. It will immensely help the reader if he bears
in mind the following few words which the Holy prophet gave expression to : "I was the light with God
the High, before Adam was made, by two thousand
years. This light was praising the glory of God
the High, so were the angels with His glorification,
so that when God the High made Adam He put

this light in his clay and God sent me down towards the earth in Adam's back; and bore me up in the ark in Noah's back; and put me in the back of Abraham, the friend of God, when he was thrown towards the fire: and he continued to transfer me from sacred backs towards pure and high pedigreed womb until He brought me out between my two parents in Holy wedlock." He also said "I am the prayer of my father Abraham." It is the evolution of this light and the fulfilment of this prayer mentioned by the venerable benefactor of humanity that had a mystic influence over the majority of population of the surface of the globe to embrace the folds of the religion of peace.

## HIS MARRIAGE

When the purity and honesty of his life began to be generally known, Al-Amin had been entrusted by Khadija binte Khwalid, descended like himself from Kossay, with a commercial enterprise to Syria in return for a share in the profits of the venture. She also sent a slave of her own to accompany him. Muhammad executed his commission with such deligence and honesty that the venture resulted in a far larger profit than Khadija had expected. His kindness and courtesy won the heart of Khadija's slave and on returning to Mecca he gave a full account of the purity and nobility of Muhammad's life to Khadija who was so effected by the recital that she offered her hand in marriage to Muhammad and was accepted by him. He was twenty-five and she was forty. But it was a union of two souls. There never was a better husband or a more faithful wife. He had by her three sons—the first one being named Kassim, and hence the Holy Prophet is called Abul Kassim (the father of Kassim)—and four daughters. Fournately or unfortunately, all the three sons were taken away from him while they were young. Soon after his marriage he formed a league or society called the League of Fusul, by which the principal members of the family of Zuhra or Faym bound themselves by a Solemn oath to defend every individual, whether Meccan or stranger, free or slave, from the wrongs and injustices of the wicked within Meccan territories and to obtain redress for the wrongs already done. Thus was the prayer of Abraham being fulfiled even before Muhammad (peace be upon him) was proclaimed prophet by the order of God. The Nur (light) was gradually unfolding itself. This light of God may most appropriately be called the "Liberator" of all mankind, for it was through him that all the shackles of prejudice, impiety, oppression, and slavery, both physical and spiritual, were torn asunder for ever. Whatever spiritual progress has been made in this world since his time is due directly and indirectly to the influence of the illumination which he brought into this world.

## EMANCIPATION OF THE SLAVES.

This first act of Khadeeja, after her marriage with Muhammad was that she put the whole of her wealth, including her slaves, at the disposal of Muhammad who immediately set all the slaves at liberty, and thus accomplished in his youth that which aged leaders had been unable to accomplish during long life times, *viz*. to strike a fatal blow at the root of slavery, in a town where the institution of slavery was the foundation of the entire social fabric and was indispensabe to its working.

## THE REBUILDING OF THE KAABA.

In the year A. C. 605, when he was thirtyfive years of age, the Koresh resolved to rebuild the Kaaba, which had been destroyed by fire some years before. The veneration for this ancient house caused such mutual jealousies that when the work had advanced to the required height for placing the famous Black Stone it was stopped. All the branches of Koresh disputed the honour of placing this stone in its proper position. The men of two branches of the tribe having resolved to maintain their pretension against all others, plunged their hands

in a vase full of blood and swore to die rather than
to yield   The work was suspended and an assembly was convened inside the Kaaba to devise means
to avoid the civil war which was imminent   This
controversy was entrusted to the arbitration of an
aged Koresh who proposed that the first person who
entered the enclosure where the assembly was
being held should be deemed a fit person to put the
black stone in its proper place.   Everyone agreed
to this proposal, and whilst all eyes were fixed on
the entrance, Lo! who should enter but Muhammad,
"the praised one" (on him be peace) the Trustworthy, the Defender of the weak against the
strong, the Liberator of mankind, the Light of God.
He laid out a mantle on the ground, chose four persons
who where the most influential men amongst the
four principal branches of Koresh, and made each one
hold one side of the mantle, on which he put the
Black Stone ; and when the mantle had been raised
to a convenient height, Muhammad with his own
hands, put the stone in its hole in the wall and thus
whilst conciliating the contention of the rival parties, he himself took the most active part in the
work.   Is there anyone, Muslim or non-Muslim,
who fails to see the hand of God working in this
rebuilding of the Kaaba ? In kissing the Black
Stone or its remnants to-day, either by touching it
with their fingers or symbolically from a distance,

the Muslims are kissing the hand of the Holy Prophet who laid it there.

Let us now have a look at the moral state of Arabia at this time. The Arabs of the time of Muhammad were pagans pure and simple; without any government except their tribal ties, without any arts or culture except poetry of the most boastful . swagger ; and without any history except the glorification of their genealogies. There was the Kaaba, of course, the house of God built by Abraham and Ishmael for the worship of One God, but this very Kaaba had become the centre of all Arab idolatories. each tribe had its own divinity and own particular idol. which it worshipped. It is said that there were 365 idols inside the Kaaba—an idol for every day of the year. The only occupation of the Arabs was inter-tribal war, and their wealth consisted solely of their flocks of sheep and camel. They were addicted to gambling, to unrestricted polygamy, incest, wars of revenge, burying alive their female children as being so many useless mouths to feed in times of want and scaricity ; brigandage and rapine went hand in hand with hospitality to the stranger. They had a most complex and highly inflexional language, but barring this qulification they were not different from the worst savages, living on the surface of the earth, and morally they were worse than most

savages. And these were the descendants of
Abraham whom God had ordered to rebuild the
Kaaba. "And when his Lord taught Abraham",
says Allah, "certain words, and he accomplished
learning them, He said, 'I will make thee a leader
unto men! Replied Abraham, 'and from my seed?'
He said, 'But my covenant includes not the unjust.'

## HIS LIFE OF RETIREMENT AND CONTEMPLATION

A contemplation of the ills that effected his
country made him sad, and he wanted to retire to a
cave at the top of a mountain called Hira, three
miles from Mecca, where he used to ponder over the
condition of his country and the prevalence of
polytheism and devoted himself to the worship of
the "One Eternal God", revealed by God to
Moses in these words.—And God spoke all these
words saying "I *am* the Lord Thy God which have
brought Thee out of the hand of Egypt, out of the
house of bondage.—Thou shalt have no other God
before me". (Exodus 20 : 1, 2 and 3). He found such
comfort in the latter occupation, that he often carried with him provision sufficient to sustain him
over several days and spent long periods of time in
a cave in the worship and contemplation of the
Almighty.

## THE FIRST REVELATION

At last when he arrived in the fortieth year he received divine revelation to the following effect : "Worship one God and Pray to Him alone for Spiritual and intellectual advancement and for the acquisition of such learning as has not previously been revealed to mankind " When he received this revelation he felt troubled and proceeded home, and related the whole incident to his wife, at the same time expressing his fear that God meant to try him. Khadeeja, who used to study every movement of his with affectionate solicitude, comforted him and said, "Nay God will surely not try thee, for thou dost behave kindly towards thy relatives, dost assist the helpless, thus exhibit the most excellent moral qualities, dost entertain thy guests hospitably and dost help those who have been overtaken by misfortune." This was the testimony of a woman who was his wife, and was, therefore, familiar with the minutest details of his life. There could be no better or truer of his character. For, the real nature of a man can be judged only by experience, and nobody can have greater experience of the nature of a man than his own wife. Muhammad was not however, wholly comforted by what his wife had said, and she therefore suggested that he should go to her cousin, who was a Biblical scholar, and should enquire from him the significance of this revelation. Accordingly he went to Warka-bin-Naufal, who was his wife's cousin and told him of his experience. Waraky replied "Be not troubled. Thou hast received revelation from God in the same manner in which Moses use to receive it," and added, "I grieve over my old age, I wish I were younger and could witness the day when God will appoint thee for the guidance of mankind. I am afraid thy people will drive thee forth from thy home". Muhammad who used to spend every hour of his life thinking over the welfare of his people and of mankind, and who was extremely popular with his townsmen, was surprised to hear this and exclaimed in wonder, "will my people indeed drive me forth?" Warka replied, "that they surely will. No man has ever been entrusted with a message so vital as thou hast been entrusted with, but his people have oppressed and persecuted him". In view of the love which he bore to his people, the affection which he displayed towards everyone of his townsmen, and the services which he rendered to the poor, the intelligence that he would be driven forth by his people came as a surprise to him. But the future held greater surprises in store for him.

### HIS CALL FOR MINISTRY.

Within a month of this incident he again received a revelation in which he was commanded to

-call mankind to God to abolish all forms of polytheism, or idoltry, to supress evil and transgression,
and to establish purity and righteousness in the
world. That the holy prophet is a descendent of
Ishmael son of Abraham the faithful is an unques-
tioned fact of universal acceptence. As to the proof
of Muhammad's prophetic mission, there are as many
evidences outside Islamic history as in it. The Holy
Bible, the authorised scripture of the civilized
world, in Genesis 17 : 20 says "And as for Ishmael I
have heard him; behold I have blessed him and will
make him fruitful and will multiply him exceeding-
ly ; twelve princes shall he beget and I will make
him a great nation". The lineage of Ishmael is
abundantly blessed and thus the Holy promise is
fulfilled to its last word as one third of the population of the globe are his descendents. In Solomon's
Song 5 : 10 to 16 we find "My beloved is white and
ruddy the chiefest among the ten thousand . ." This
verse and several other succeeding ones descriptive
of his features and identification might have
stealthily escaped the notice of every Bible reader
but the actual significance of the words "beloved"
and "Chiefest among the ten thousand" leads us to
assume that God selected one man and he was the
head of an army of ten thousand and to locate his
whereabouts we have to read Duet 33 : 2. "And he
said—the Lord came from Sinai and rose up from

Seir unto them ; he shined forth from mount Pharan
and he came with ten thousand of saints; from his
right hand went a fiery law for them". Habakkuk
3 : 3. "God came from Teman and the Holy one from
Mount Pharan. Selah, His glory covered the
heavens and the earth was full of his priase".

These two verses supply us sufficient information to establish the fact that the aforesaid "beloved and chief of ten thousand" should come
from Pharan. Jesus Christ is the last prophet
from the line of Israelites or more commonly
known as David's house and certainly Jesus hails
from Bethlehem and the unfulfilled promise of
the almighty God with Abraham has been meter-
ialised in the creation of a prophet (Muhammad)
who came from Pharan risen from the seed of
Ishmael. The person in whom these three conditions are fulfiled must necessarily be the prophet
selected. Muhammadium is the original hebrew
word for "beloved" and it is Muhammad that came
from Pharan with ten thousand while the word
Pharan (Arabic and Hebrew) means "two run-
aways" namely Hagar and Ishmael and eventually
the place was named after them which is visited
annually by millions of the faithful even to this
day. Lastly fiery laws were framed by Muhammad,
as such stern laws were found absolutely necessary
in those dark ages to mould the vindictive character

of the barbarous Arabs. Muhammad came with ten
thousand to conquer the city of black stone ɪ 'e.
Kaaba. This black stone around which surrounds
mystery and history of several centuries while hope
and faith of the millions of muslims dazzle over it,
was fixed by King Solomon in the temple of Jerusalem which was later on fixed in Kaaba at Mecca
where it now remains to carry away our immagination through several mystified accounts to the dark
ages where the light of God was shedding out its
golden beams.

This revelation conferred on him the rank of
Prophet, and in him was thus fulfilled the Prophecy
contained in Deutronomy, 18-18 where it is written
"I will raise them up a Prophet from among their
brethren like unto thee" Muhammad was a descendent of Ishmael and was thus a cousin of the Israelites, and he was, like Moses, the bearer of a New
Law. The moment he was raised to prophet-hood,
however, the whole world changed for him. Those
that had loved him previously now hated him,
those that had praised him now disparaged him,
and those that had previously comforted him began
now to persecute him.

### ABU-BAKER JOINS HIM.

But four persons who had opportunities of
coming into the closest contact with him believed

in him. These where Khadeeja his wife, Ali the son
of Abu Talih, his cousin, Zaid his freedman, and Abu-
Baker his dearest friend, and the ground of their belief was that Muhammad could not possibly be an
imposter. The manner in which Abu-Baker signified
his acceptance of Muhammad as a Prophet was signi-
ficant. When the latter received the revelation com-
manding him to proclaim his prophetic mission, Abu-
Baker was sitting in the house of a Nobleman of
Mecca. A maid came into the room and exclaimed,
"I wonder what is the matter with Khadeeja today.
She says her husband is a Prophet as Moses was a
Prophet". At this those present began to laugh, and
described such a claim as the result of madness. Abu
Baker, however, who knew Muhammad intimately
immediately left the place, and proceeding to the
latter's house, enquired whether he had put forward
any claim. Muhammad replied that God had appointed him for the guidance of mankind and for estab-
lishing the Unity of God. On hearing this, and without asking any further questions, Abu Baker exclaimed "I Swear by my father and my mother that
thou hast never uttered a falsehood, and I cannot
conceive that thou wouldst say that concerning
God which is not true. I bear witness, therefore,
that there is no God besides Allah, and that thou art
the messenger of God." There after Abu Baker
began to exhort several young men who respected

him for the purity of the life, and presently seven of these young men accepted Muhammad.

## PERSECUTION.

It is not an easy thing to accept the truth. The people of Mecca, whose principle means of livelihood was the guardianship and services of idol temples, could not be expected to tolerate the doctrine that there were none worthy of worship except God. As soon as the relatives of those who had become Muslims became aware of this fact, they began to persecute them. Usman's uncle secured his body with a rope and confined him to a room in the house, declaring that he would not release him until he had repented of his new faith. Another young Muslim, Zubair, who was only fifteen years of age was also imprisoned by his relatives, and the latter used to fill the chamber in which Zubair was confined with smoke, in order to make him recant, but he remained firm and did not cease to profess his faith. A new form of persecution was invented by the mother of another young Muslim. She refused to take any food until he reverted to the faith of his ancestors. He replied that he was willing to obey his parents in all temporal matters, but that he could not obey them contrary to the pleasure of God, as the allegiance which he owed to God was higher than that which he owed to his parents. In short, with the exception of Abu Baker and Khadeeja, those who believed in the Holy Prophet in the beginning, were all young men between fifteen and twenty years age. It may be said that Muhammad, being an orphan, had from an early age learnt to carve out his own path, and that when God raised him to prophet-hood the first who gathered round him were young people. With reference to its early history, therefore, Islam may be described as the religion of the young.

### HIS MANNER OF APPROACH.

As a prophet is bound to convey his message generally to those for whom it is meant, Muhammad adopted the following mode for this purpose. One day he took his stand on a rising piece of ground and started calling upon the principal houses in Mecca. As the people reposed great trust and confidence in him they began to gather round him in answer to his call, and those who could not come themselves sent representatives to listen to what he had to say. "Ye people of Mecca, if I were to tell you that a great army is advancing upon Mecca and has arrived close to it, intending to attack it, would you beleive me?". Now this was apparently impossible, for Mecca was regarded as a sacred town by the Arabs, and it could not be conceived that any tribe would march against it. Besides, the Meccan shepards used to graze their flocks all round Mecca for long distances, and in the event of an army advancing towards Mecca they would have speedily warned the people of the danger. Yet the answer which they all made to Muhammad's question on this occasion was, "We would believe thee, for thou hast never been guilty of a falsehood." To this the Holy Prophet rejoined, "You testify that I never speak that which is not true. I inform you, therefore, that God has appointed me to deliver his message to you, and to point out to you the error of your ways. The moment the people heard this they ran away from him, and exclaimed that the man was either mad or an imposter.

## ILL-TREATMENT OF HIS FOLLOWERS

This incident created a sensation in Mecca, and those who had already believed in him were subjected to severer persecution than before. Brothers were deserted by brothers, children were driven out by their parents, and slaves were tortured by their masters. Persecutions assumed several forms. Young men who cared little for customs and traditions and judged religious questions by the test of reason, and, therefore, were quick to accept the truth of the Holy Prophet, were imprisoned and starved by their parents, in the hope that they might renounce their faith. Such measure, however failed to shake them, and they continued to worship their Maker with dry lips and sunken eyes, till their parents, fearing that they might be starved to death supplied them with food. Pity was sometimes taken upon these young men, but the case of those slaves and poor people who had become Muslims, but who had nobody to protect or to help them, was indeed pitiful. Slaves were made to wear steel armour and then stand in the burning sun of Arabia till their skins were scorched. Some were dragged along the burning sands by means of ropes tied to their legs, the bodies of others were seared with red-hot irons. One form of turture was to puncture the bodies of muslims with needles. A devote muslim lady was killed by a spear being run through her body. But these and other un-speakable horrers were borne unflichingly by the Muslims and even under torture they did not cease to declare that they could not relinquish the worship of One God. The Holy Prophet himself was the victim of persecution, but in his case the conduct of his enemies was influenced by un-willingness to give offence to his family, which was universally respected in Mecca. Nevertheless, he was often abused and ashes and rubbish were thrown upon him when he used to be prostrate in prayer. Once when he was in this position an enemy of his placed his foot upon his neck and kept him pinned in that position for a long time. On one occasion when he went to the Mosque for prayers a cloth was put round his neck, and an attempt was made to strangle him by twisting the cloth.

## HIS TEACHINGS.

In spite of all this opposition the Holy Prophet continued his propaganda. Wherever he found a few men sitting together he would go and teach them that God was One, that there was no other God besides Him, neither in Heaven nor on Earth; that He had neither son nor daughter; He begat not, nor was he begotten; that they should put their faith in Him and worship Him and pray to Him alone: that He was free from all grossness and therefore could not be perceived by our physica eyes; that he was the Master of all Powers who nad created the Universe, and that the souls of the dead returned to Him and were given new life; men should love him and strive to attain nearness to Him that they should purify their hearts, tongues and their actions; that they should eschew falsehood, murder disturbance, theft. robbery, false charge,

faultfinding, abuse, transgression and envy: that
they should not spend their time in the pursuit of
luxury and the satisfaction of their desires, but
should devote themselves to the service and welfare
of mankind, and should promote love and peace in
the world.

## PAGAN BELIEFS OF HIS COUNTRYMEN.

This is what he taught, and yet the people
laughed at him. The people of Mecca were
confirmed idol-worshippers and their temple contained hundreds of idols whom they daily
worshipped and before whom men made offerings,
which were the means of support of many respectable
familes. To them the doctrine of worship of one
God alone appeard fanatic. They could not understand why God could not incarnate himself in man
or an idol. They could not reconcile themselves
to the idea of an Invisible God. Therefore they
laughed at the Holy Prophet whenever they saw
him, and exclaimed, "behold this man has combined
all the Gods into one" for they imagined that the
separate existence of many Gods was an incontro-
vertible fact, and that when Muhammad taught
that there was only one God, he meant that, he had
combined all the Gods into one. They ascribed
their own fantastic notions to the Holy Prophet,
and then laughed at their absurdity. The doctrine

of a life after death furnished them with another
source of merriment. They were amused at the
idea that the dead would be made to live again.

## REFUGEES TO ABYSSINIA.

When the persecution of the Muslims at Mecca
became unbearable the Holy Prophet permitted his
companions to take refuge in Abyssinia, which was
even then ruled by a Christian King. The majority
of Muslims, men and women, therefore, left their
homes in Mecca and proceeded to Abyssinia. The
hostility of the Meccans however, pursued them
hither, and the latter sent a deputation to the king
of Abyssinia that he should handover the fugitives
to the Meccans. But this Christian King was a
monarch who loved to be just. When he had heard
of the deputation he desired to hear the other side,
and the Muslims were commended to appear before
him. It was a pathetic scene. The muslims who
had been compelled to leave their homes as the
result of persecution by their own men appeared
before the King of Abyssinia, apprehensive that
they would be handed over to the Meccans and
would be subjected by them to torture severer than
those which they had experienced before. The king
enquired from them why they had come to this
country. Their spokesman replied "Your Majesty,

we were ignorant and had no knwledge of good or
evil. We worshipped idols and were unaware of the
Unity of God. All manner of evil was prevalent
among us; transgression, robbery, murder and
fornication were not counted as faults. God then
raised Muhammad (on whom be peace and the
blessing of God) as a prophet among us. He taught
us the worship of the One God, restrained us from
evil-doing, enjoined justness and fairness, exhorted
us to love each other, and guided us along the path
of purity and righteousness. Therefore our brethren
began to persecute us and inflicted various tortures
upon us, till we were compelled to leave our homes
and take refuge in your country. These people have
followed us here and demand our return. Our
only fault is that we worship the one Eternal God."
The King was so affected by this reply that he
refused to hand over the Muslims to the Meccans.
The latter then intrigued with the Court nobles and
the next day reiterated their demand, stating that
the Muslims were in the habit of abusing Jesus.
The King again summoned the Muslims and they
explained to him what Islam taught concerning
Jesus, viz. that he was a beloved servant of God and
a prophet, but that they would not accept him as
God, as God was only One. At this the nobles
were excited and demanded that the King should
punish the Muslims. The King, however, replied
that his own belief concerning Jesus was the same

as that held by the Muslims, and that he could not, on account of that belief, hand them over to their oppressors. He told the nobles that he did not mind their resentment, as he preferred the pleasure of God, to the sovereignity of his country.

## HARD TIMES AT MECCA.

In Mecca the persecution of the Holy Prophet himself was increasing. The Meccans approached his uncle Abu Talib, who was one of the chiefs of his people and fear of whom restrained them from proceeding to extremes against the Holy Prophet. and suggested that he should adopt the son of some other chief, and should hand cver Muhammad to their vengeance. S₁id Abu Talib "This is indeed a strange request. You wish me to hand over my property to one of your brats, and to hand over my nephew to be tortured to death by you. Would even an animal kills its own and love those of another?" Dis-appointed in this they asked him to restrain his nephew from preaching the Unity of God and the iniquity of idol-worship. Thereupon Abu Talib sent for Muhammad and asked him whether he could not please the chief man of Mecca by conforming to their wishes. He replied, "Uncle I owe you a deep debt of gratitude, but even for your own sake I cannot forsake God. If you are afraid of the hostility of the people, you may leave me to myself, but I must preach the Truth which God has revealed to me. I cannot sit silent and witness the ruin of my people.

## THE TEMPTING OFFERS.

The Meccans next resorted to cajolery and entreaty. They deputed a chief to approach the Holy Prophet and to request him not to disturb the peace of the town, suggesting at the same time that if his object was to gain honour, they were willing to acclaim him as the most honoured citizen of Mecca ; if he desired wealth, they were ready to make him the wealthiest citizen of Mecca by making up a large contribution for him ; if he sought to set himself up as a king, they were willing to recognize him as such ; if he desired wife, he would be given the choice of all the women of Mecca ; but that he should desist from preaching the Unity of God. Hearing this the Holy Prophet replied, "If you set the sun on my right hand and the moon on my left, I shall not renounce the doctrine". Of the oneness and unity of God eighty men had so far joined the Holy Prophet, (on whom be peace and blessing of God).

## BLOCKADE AND BOYCOTT.

When, however, the rumours of the doings at Mecca spread into the country, people began to arrive in Mecca to find out for themselves what all this meant. The Meccans were chagrined at this, and the streets were picketted to prevent anybody from seeing the Holy Prophet. At the same time they resolved to put an end to his life. Learning this, his uncle and his other relatives withdrew with him into a neighbouring valley in order the better to be able to protect him.

Frustrated in their designs, the Meccans entered into a covenant and to boycott the Holy Prophet, the members of his family and all the Muslims. People were forbidden to sell articles of food or clothing to them and inter-marriage and every other kind of intercourse with them was prohibited, unless they agreed to hand over the Holy Prophet to the Meccans to be dealt with by the latter as they pleased. Mecca is a lonely town in the desert. There is no other town within forty miles of it. It may, therefore, be imagined what hardships the Muslims and the relatives of the Holy Prophet had to undergo as the result of this boycott. Pickets were posted to prevent any person from supplying them with food or drink, and this state of affairs lasted for three years. They had to watch for favourable opportunities at night to bring in provisions which were very often completely exhausted, and they had to subsist for days on the leaves and bark of trees. A companion of the Holy Prophet relates that the Muslims looked haggard and emaciated and their health began to suffer. Not for days or for weeks, but for three whole years was this greatest benefactor of humanity persecuted in this manner for preaching the worship of one God and the acquisition of high qualities, but neither his own sufferings nor those of his followers and dear ones interfered with his high and noble purpose. After three years of continuous persecution the tardy humanity of some of the Meccan chiefs rebelled against this tyranny and they tore up the covenant into which they had entered. The Holy Prophet and his companions then left the valley into which they had withdraw, but his old uncle and his faithful wife could not escape the effects of this long period of persecution, and died shortly after.

## HIS JOURNEY TO TAIF.

They say, "Love is blind." It does not see which way lies danger or safety. Muhammad (peace be upon him) is a lover of mankind. The Meccan chiefs have rejected him, tortured him, persecuted his faithful followers ; his sons are in their graves ; his

wife is dead; his uncle Abu Talib is no more. What
is he to do? He goes to Taif and calls the people there
to the right path—the path of everlasting happiness.
His life companion, Zaid, follows his master. The
hooligans of Taif, like beasts, set upon him. They
cut his heart with their abusive tongues, they stone
him till his shoes are full of blood, and they drive
him out of their town into the desert till it is dark.
Let him perish there or live as he may. And does
he curse them or abuse them or do any of the other
thousand and one things that ordinary mortals
under such circumstances are apt to do? No. He
has a long heart-to-heart talk with the Almighty.
The last few sentences of his prayers are here for
our guidance. He is guiding us here. His light is
all round us. He says "O Lord these people know
not that what I tell them is the truth, they are doing
these because they think it is right. Be not angry
with them therefore and send not down punishment
upon them but open their eyes to the truth and
enable them to accept it. I make my complaint
unto thee, out of my feebleness and the vanity of
my wishes. I am insignificant in the sight of men.
O Thou merciful. Lord of the weak. Thou art my
Lord. Do not forsake me. Leave me not a prey
to strangers, nor to mine enemies. If thou art not
offended, I am safe. I seek refuge in the light of
Thy countenance, by which all darkness is dispersed, and peace come here and hereafter. Let not

Thy anger descend on me; solve my difficulties as it pleaseth Thee. There is no power, no help, but in Thee." His prayer is always accepted. In fact, Allah has already spoken to him :—

,'By the forenoon (when the sun is high) and by the night when it spreads, thy Lord has not forsaken thee (O Muhammad) nor is He displeased with thee; and God will bestow His favours on thee so that thou shalt be pleased". And how this is done is shown by the result of his life. Maltreated by the Meccans, stoned by the street Arabs of Taif, Muhammad is accepted by the visitors from Madina.

### HIS FLIGHT TO MADINA

In A. C. 622 the twelfth year of his mission, seventy five representatives of Yathreb (which is now known as Madina) came to invite him to their city, and Muhammad pledged himself to go to them and not to abandon them whatever may happen. When the Meccans saw that his doctrine was beginning to spread outside Mecca, they hit upon a novel plan of putting an end to his life. They selected one man from each tribe to make a united assault upon him during the night and to finish him, thus making all tribes responsible for the outrage, so that the clan of the Holy Prophet, even if

they resented it, should feel themselves helpless
against the united tribes of Mecca. The Holy Prophet had, however, been warned of the danger by
God, he left Mecca the same night and he left his
son-in-law Ali on his bed and escaped through the
window and reached Yathreb (the city of the Prophet) in June 622. This is the Hejira or flight
And now begins a new era of which the present
year is the 1350. The people of Madina readily
accepted his doctrine and within a short time
almost all of them became Muslims. They chose
the Holy Prophet as their King, and thus the cor-
ner-stone which the builders of his town "had
rejected" became the crown of the state of
Madina.

## ELECTED KING OF MADINA.

As king of Madina also, his occupation was the
teaching and instruction of the people, and he
never gave up his simple mode of life. He spent his
time in calling men to the worship of one God and
teaching them the moral and social ordinances of
Islam. He personally lead the five daily prayers
in the Mosque, settled all disputes that arose
among the members of the community, and devoted time and attention to the promotion of national
welfare, for instance, in matters relating to

commerce, education and hygiene. He paid special
attention to the circumstances and needs of the poor,
and strove to fulfil the latter. For instance, he
would sometimes run errands for the poor who stood
in need of such service. During his many occupa-
tions he yet found time to join in games and pas-
times to the young and encouraged in them the
development of a healthy national spirit. When he
returned to his home he often assisted his wives in
household work. At midnight when everybody
had retired to rest, he would leave his bed and
spend the still and dark hours in the worship of his
Maker, till sometimes his feet were swollen as the
result of standing in an attitude of devotion.

## HIS MESSAGE MAY BRIEFLY BE DESCRIBED AS FOLLOWS.

1. He taught that God is One, and all other beings, whether angels or men, are His creatures; and
that it is offering an insult to God to imagine that
He incarnates himself in man or in idols, or that He
begets or is begotten. He is above all such contin-
gencies. He alone gives life and He alone takes
it away. All reformers and Prophets were His
servants, and none of them possessed Divine Power.
All men should worship Him alone, and should put
their trust in Him alone.

*Object Of Man's Creation*

2. He taught that God has created man for the highest spiritual, moral, intellectual and social advancement, and that in order to fulfil this object, He has constantly raised Prophets among all nations. He repudiated the doctrine that Prophethood had been confined to any particular nation, for this would involve a charge of partiality against the Creator and would amount to a denial of His Providence. He testified to the truth of the Prophets of all nations.

3. He taught that the word of God has been revealed in all ages to the respective needs of the times, and he claimed that God had appointed him for the guidance of this last age. Accordingly, he taught that the Quran was a more perfect code of laws than the previously revealed books and he called all mankind to it.

### The Eternal Word

4. He taught that God always speaks to His servants and reveals signs in their support, to assure them of His existence and of His Love and he claimed that those who followed his teachings would perceive the truth of these things within themselves.

## LIFE OF PEACE.

5. He taught that in spite of differences of
religion, people ought to live in  peace  and  amity
with each other and should not quarrel over religious
matters.  For if a man has the truth  he need  not
quarrel over it, he had but to present it and it  will
of itself conquer the  hearts  of  the  people.  He,
therefore, permitted  even  Christians  to  conduct
their service in his Mosques—an  instance of large-
hearted tolerance which is hardly to  be  met  with
even in this advanced twentieth century.

## INTER-DEPENDENCE OF THE SPIRITUAL AND
## THE PHYSICAL.

6. He emphasised that man's life has two
aspects, the spiritual aspect and the physical aspect,
and thus they were so  related  to  each  other  that
they could not  be separated from  each  other,  and
that each of them reacts upon the  other.  He  laid
special stress upon  the  truth  that  no  amount  of
outward conformity  to  religious  injuctions  could
avail in the absence of the  purity of the heart, and
that, on the other hand the mind could not be trained and developed without the help  of outward conformity.  For a  perfect  development  of  man,
therefore, it is necessary that regard must be had for
both these aspects.

## MORALITY.

7. In respect of morals, he taught that all men are born with pure and untainted natures, and whatever corruption appears can be directly attributed to faulty education or wrong upbringing. That is why he always insisted on the high education and high upbringing.

## SELF-PURIFICATION.

8 He used to emphasise the fact, too, that the real object of good morals is the true transformation of one's self as well as others. He would not stress one aspect of a question alone, he would keep in view all sides of things. He would never say, for instance, that one should make use of mercy and forgiveness on every occasion. He would say, that if one was harmed or injured by another, one should think how best one could improve the character of a harmer or injurer. If he happens to be a nobleminded person, he would certainly mend in future if he was given an opportunity to do so. So he would say such a person deserves every consideration of mercy and forgiveness. But if he happens to be so degraded as to misinterpret your forgiving him as a sign of weakness, or fear and thus becomes bolder and more impudent, in his wickedness, then it is time that strict measures were

adopted, or else he would harm others besides your-self. Punish him according to the measure of his guilt or else innocent and weak people would suffer for no fault of their own.

## HIS TEACHINGS AS TO WARS.

9. He taught that offensive wars should never be undertaken. War was permitted only as a defensive measure. Even in the latter case, if the aggressing party repents of its folly and is willing to come to terms you should be ready to enter into peace.

10. Again he taught that the spirit or soul of a man is created immortal, therefore with the death of the body there is no death to it. It would continue making its progress without undergoing any annihilation. So much so, that even sinners and the iniquitous, after undergoing purificatory chastisement and after they are purged of all evil inclinations, will share the eternal Mercy of Allah and they will be placed on the road of eternal pro-gress again.

## THE MECCAN HOSTILITY.

When the Meccans saw that he had secured a good opportunity of spreading his teachings among the inhabitants of Madina and many people had begun to join his fold, they led many expeditions against him, but all these military attempts failed. Even here his superiority over them was clearly demonstrated, for in spite of the heavy preparations on their part and the odds being in their favour, sometimes they numbered thrice as many as the Muslims—they were always defeated, which was very unusual. The Muslims were victorious and the Meccans were helplessly discomfitted. Sometimes the Muslims did suffer some sort of check or repulse, but it was never a defeat in the real sense of the word, for ultimately it led to an overwhelming defeat of the enemy.

These campaigns on the part of the enemy led to very clear and direct results. One was that out of all this turmoil he emerged the supreme King of Arabia. Secondly, he had occasion during this time of strife and stress to exhibit some of those high moral traits which could but only be shown during war and fight. This established his moral superiority still further. At the same time this stress and strife proved to the world what a spirit of sacrifice and devotion he had infused into his followers.

For the sake of illustration I relate here a few episodes of the battles of Badr, Ohud and Honain.

The Holy Prophet sets himself to reform the nation and makes a pact with the Jews and Christians, granting them equal rights of protection and

worship with the Muslims, and all are to defend
Madina and to act in union, with perfect equality
and justice under God.   Henceforth he is the prophet
of God, by God's command the protector of the lives
and property of Muslims and Jews and Christians
in and round Madina, by agreement.   He is both
the prophet of God and the President of a State.
The Jews are not willing to see Muhammad (peace
be on him) being recognized the prophet of God.
They make common cause with the Koresh of
Mecca, and before the Holy Prophet has been a year
at Madina, the Meccans more than a thousand
strong, under Abu Jahal (The father of Ignorance),
invade his territory and are met by three hundred
Muslims at Badr.   The three hundred faithful
vanquished over a thousand infidels.   Abu Jahal is
killed in a battle, his followers flee and are killed
or made prisioner.

Three years after his immigration from Mecca
the enemy with three thousand soldiers set out of
Mecca to attack Madina.   Madina is two hundred
miles away from Mecca, but the enemies were so
confident of their success that they advanced into
the very neighbourhood of Madina. At Ohud, which
is only eight miles away from Madina, the Holy
prophet marched out with one thousand men
to meet them.   One of his bands misunderstood
his directions, and the result was that victory which

was almost theirs was turned into a defeat. In spite
of the fact that the Muslims were victorious on all
the fronts, yet owing to that tactical blunder the
enemy turned upon them and during the course of
the battle at one time the situation developed so
critical that the Muslims were driven far behind, so
far, indeed, that the Holy Prophet was left alone in
circle of his bitterest foes.  At this moment he stood
so firm that though his men had fallen back
he would not return a single step. When the
Muslims realised this state of affairs, they made a
determined effort to come to his help, but only
fourteen of them could break through the enemy's
lines to him.  At that time the Holy Prophet was
struck with a stone and he received a wound in
the head and fell down in a swoon.  He was burn-
ed under the dead bodies of the Muslims who fell
defending him.  It was generally thought that the
Holy Prophet had received his martyrdom.  His
followers were like so many lovers when they heard
the news : many of them threw down their arms on
the field of battle and began to cry.  One of the
Muslim soldiers who was not aware of the rumour,
and happened to pass by, enquired the cause of this
despair.  When informed of the reported death of
the Holy Prophet, the soldier remarked that now
was the time for a more desperate fight.  " We
shall follow our beloved leader to death."  Having
said this, he drew his sword and fell upon the enemy

and was killed; seventy wounds were found on his body when it was discovered later on.

When the body of the Holy Prophet was discovered under the dead bodies of his followers, it was found that he was alive. The news spread and the Muslim army began to rally again, and the enemy was routed. A Muslim soldier missed one of his relatives, so he went out in search of him. He found him severely wounded and at his last breath. As soon as the wounded man saw his friend, he enquired of him of the welfare of the Holy Prophet and when he was told that the Holy Prophet was safe, his face beamed with delight and he said "NOW I die happy." Then the dying man caught hold of his relative's hand and requested him to convey the following message to his dear and near ones: "Muhammad the Prophet of God is a charge in our hands for which we are answerable to God. It is your duty to protect this divine charge. Take heed you should fall short of your duty." This is how the Muslims even evinced their faithfulness towards the Holy Prophet. The Muslim ladies were in no way behind their men in this respect. When news reached Madina that the Holy Prophet was killed, the Madinites to the last soul left the city for the battlefield with hearts full of grief and sorrow They were met by the Muslim army, which was returning from the battlefield delighted with the Prophet safe among them. A women went forward and asked one of the soldiers, "How is the Holy Prophet?" As the man knew the Holy Prophet was quite safe, he did not care to answer her question, but said "Your father is killed, madam". " How is the Prophet of God?" she said with impatience, "I do not enquire of you about the death of my father," Again the man did not care to set her anxiety about the Holy Prophet at rest, and replied, "Your two brothers are killed, dear sister." She lost her patience and said with sternness, "I do not ask you to tell me anything about the fate of my brothers. Would you or would you not let me know how is the Prophet of God?" "The Holy Prophet is quite safe," replied the man. "God be praised, " she exclaimed, "if the prophet of God lives, then the whole world lives, and I do not care who else". How could such sincere devotion and genuine attachment for the person of the Holy Prophet exist in the hearts of his followers without a pure and perfect example and a keen solicitude for the welfare of mankind on his part? .

## THE HONAIN EPISODE AND THE PROPHETIC CHARGE.

Similarly the Muslim army was once marching through a mountain-pass on both sides of which the archers of the enemy lay concealed. The Muslims were quite unaware of the position of the enemy, who began to throw arrows at them. This sudden onslaught frightened the horses and the camels of the Muslims, and the riders lost control over them. The Holy Prophet was left with only sixteen companions amidst a host of 4,000 archers, and rest of the Muslim army was dispersed. The Holy Prophet quite undaunted, advanced his horse towards the enemy's ranks. Seeing this, the handful of companions that were with him were disconserted, and dismounting from their horses, held the reins of his horse and said. 'The enemy is advancing triumphantly and the Muslim army has been routed, and the safety of Islam depends on your safety , please go back, so that the scattered Muslims should come together." "Leave off the reins of my horse," said the Prophet, and then exclaimed, "I am the Prophet of God, I am not a liar ; let him who can injure me." Saying these words he advanced towards the ranks of the enemy with the sixteen companions left with him. No human hand could do him any harm. Then the Prophet ordered one of the followers to call the flying Muslims with a loud voice, in these words, "Ye Medinites, the Prophet of God calls you". A companion of the Holy Prophet relates : "Our horses and camels had become terribly frightened and were running away from the field of battle, and all our efforts to restrain them and turn them back were of no avail. When we heard this call we became as if we were dead and the voice of God was calling us. I became impatient to run back. I tried to turn my camel back too, but to no purpose. The voice, "The Prophet of God calls you," was still resounding in my ears. When I saw that my camel was carrying me away from the scene of battle I took my sword out of the scabbard, killed him, and like a mad man ran towards the place from which the voice came." He writes that such was the state of all the army. He who could turn his horse or camel back to him, and he who could not do so got down off it and ran towards him. He who could not even get down, killed his animal, and hastened towards his master, and in a few minutes every one gathered round him at his call, just as the dead are said to rise up from the grave at the sound of the trumpet of Israel.

## HIS HUMANE STATUTES.

He always laid emphasis on the point that Muslims should never be the first to attack; they should, on the other hand, fight only for defence. He always enjoined upon his followers never to kill in battle women, children, clergymen, oldmen, and those who were unfit for war. He taught that those who lay down their arms should not be killed. Trees should not be cut down, buildings should not de demolished, towns and valleys should not be ravaged, and if he ever came to know that these instructions were violated he was very much displeased and became angry with the man who did so.

## HIS GENEROSITY TOWARDS THE MECCANS.

When he conquered Mecca and became King the people thereof were trembling with fear at the treatment which might be meted out to them. The residents of Madina who had not themselves seen the tortures to which the Muslims had been subjected, and had only heard of them from other people, were very much enraged at the thought of them. But when he entered Mecca he gathered together the people and said, "O ye people, I will forgive today all the wrongs which you have done to me ; ye shall not be punished." If there had been no wars and he had not been made a king, how could he become a perfect model for mankind and how could he display this aspect of human morals.

## HIS TRUE NATURE.

In short, the wars have disclosed an important aspect of his morals and demonstrated his love for peace, tranquility, forgivness and mercy because he

alone is truly merciful who had the power to show
mercy and he shows it, and he alone is worth to be
called generous who possesses riches and distributes
them. The Almighty God granted him victory
over his tyrant enemies and he forgave them all;
He granted him kingdom by his living a humble
and simple life, and by his distributing the riches
to the poor and needy.

## HIS FINAL EXHORTATIONS

In June A. C. 630 *i.e.* sixtieth year of his life,
the Holy Prophet marched with 2,000 Muslims to
Tabuk, to meet a reported invasion of the Christians
from Syria, but which, happily, does not come off
On his return to Madina, the Arabs flock from all
parts of the country offering homage and asking
for enlightenment. These embassies continue
during the next two years, A. C. 631 and 632, or
A. H. 10 and 11. Now his work is almost accomplished. He knows that, because various verses of
the Holy Quran point out to that effect. On the
25th of Zul Kaada (February 23, 632), the Prophet
leaves Madina with an immense concourse of
Muslims. On his arrival at Mecca, and before
completing all the rites of the pilgrimage, he
addresses the assembled multitude in words which
yet live in the hearts of all Muslims.

"Ye people : listen to my words, for I know not whether another year will be vouchsafed to me after this year to find myself amongst you ".

"Your lives and property are sacred and inviolable amongst one another until ye appear before the Lord, as this day and this month is sacred for all, and remember ye shall have to appear before your Lord who shall demand from you an account of all your actions . .Ye people ye have rights over your wives, and your wives, have rights over you  Treat your wives with kindness. Verily ye have taken them on security of God, and have made their persons lawful unto you by the words of God ".

"And your slaves!  See that ye feed them with such food as ye eat  yourselves, and  clothe  them with the stuff ye wear ; and if they commit a  fault which ye are not inclined to forgive, then part from them for they are the servants of the Lord, and  are not to be harshly  treated."

"Ye people listen to my words and understand the same.  Know that all Muslims are brothers unto one another.  Ye are one brotherhood.  Nothing which belongs to another is lawful unto his  brother unless freely given out of good  will.  Guard yourselves from committing injustice."

54

" Let him that is present tell it unto him that is absent  Happily he that shall be told may remember better than he who had heard it"     (Ameer Ali).

The pilgrimage is called Hajjat-ul-Balagh,  the pilgrimage of the message or Hajjat-ul-Islam.

" This is the message unto all mankind that they may be warned therewith and that they may know that  He  is  the  One  God  and  that  those possessed of understanding may remember" (Holy-Quran, Ch. 14, last verse).

He returns to Madina and at noon on  Monday, 12th Rabi-ul-awal, A. H.  11 June 8,  A. C. 632,  the Light of God leaves  the  prescribed  limits  of  the human frame and becomes for ever  Immortal,  and thus leaving behind him for the  guidance  of  the mortal world a new and  Complete  Code  of  Law called the Holy Quran and a religion of  Peace  i. e. Islam, for ever.

# CHAPTER II

## Some of the Distinctive points of Superiority of the Holy Prophet of Islam over all other Prophets.

### I. UNIVERSAL PROPHET.

HE was raised as a Prophet for the whole human race, where as the mission of all other Prophets was limited to a particular nation, country or age.

### II. PERFECT RELIGION.

He has been granted a perfect, practicable, all comprehensive and everlasting code of guidance, whereas the religions of all other Prophets suited only to the conditions prevalent in their respective ages and have no universal character.

### III. INTEGRITY OF THE REVEALED BOOK.

He alone has been given such a Book as is immune from human interpolation. The detractors of Islam could not but confess its pristine purity. For instance, such as hostile Christian writer as Sir William Muir, says . "There is probably in the world no other book which has remained twelve centuries with so pure a text".

### IV. INSPIRED REFORMERS.

He is the only Prophet whose religion (Islam) has been vouchsafed the unique Divine promise that the almighty God would raise an inspired Reformer at the beginning of every century for its revival whose duty it is to expound the real spirit of the Holy Quran. Such a Divine blessing as the above is not at all claimed by the votaries of other religious denominations.

### V. THE LIVING LANGUAGE OF THE REVEALED BOOK.

He alone has been given such a Revealed Book that the language of which (Arabic) is a living one and not dead, whereas the language of the revealed books of all other Prophets is dead.

### VI. THE LIVING GOD.

He alone has presented to the world such a Living God as speaks with his votaries in all ages, whereas the followers of all other Prophets, do not even believe that God speaks now as he spoke in the past.

## VII. SACERDOTALISM.

He stands unique among all other Divine teachers for abolishing sacerdotalism and demolishing the barriers of colour and race and stripping religious worship of expensive ceremonies.

## VIII. SCIENCE AND EDUCATION.

He stands unrivalled in giving impetus to Science and education to both the sexes.

## IX LABOUR AND CAPITAL PROBLEM SOLVED.

He is the most prominent among all other Divine Teachers in providing for the poor and the weak, by taxing the capitalists and enjoining upon the rich Muslims to pay annually compulsory alms (zakat) at the rate of $2\frac{1}{2}$ per cent on their total saving and thus left no room for Bolshevic propaganda.

## X. CHAMPION OF WOMEN'S RIGHTS.

He is the chivalrous champion of women's rights and honour and it was through him that

the world for the first time learnt that " women
have equal rights with men" and that "the
Paradise lies at the mother's feet."

## XI SLAVERY.

He is the only Prophet who has contributed
much towards the emancipation of slaves. It is
a stern fact that Muslim slaves ruled over India
as Kings, when non-Muslim world was still under
the curse of slavery.

## XII. NOBILITY OF MIND.

He displayed greatness and magnificence of
mind by his not bearing any malice or grudge
even towards his bitterest enemies who did not
spare anything in persecuting him : this was
plainly shown by his praying for their good, while
we find that Noah and Moses great prophets as they
were prayed for the destruction of their enemies.

## XIII FORGIVENESS.

He showed spirit of forgiveness to such a
degree as has no parallel in the records of human
history, not even in the annals of lives of great
prophets; this was clearly shown when he returned

to Mecca and was declared the King of Arabia : then his deadly enemies who had been thirsting for his blood were arrainged before him : their atrocities in the long period of thirteen years deserved no less retribution than death, but Lo, to the surprise of all he gave his judgement proclaiming that he freed them from all reproof that he bore no ill-will towards them and that they were to be set at liberty like free citizens. Let any one try to find such a precedent in the world's history and he will try in vain.

# CHAPTER III.

## Muhammad According To The Holy Quran

———

" MUHAMMAD is the ambassador of God; and those who believe with him are strong against those who disbelieve (in him) and are kind amongst themselves, thou seest them (O!Muhammad) bowing down and prostrating" (Holy Quran, ch. 48, v. 29). Thus has Almighty God made this light of His own a witness over our prayers and over our loves for each other, and He promises those who follow this Light an everlasting happiness.

"And those who believe and do good and believe in what has been sent down upon Muhammad, for it is the Truth from their Lord, their evils are wiped away from them and their condition is made good" (ch. 47, v. 1).

He is, however, not obeyed because he is an earthly ruler or father over a family, but simply because of his great mission and of the Master who has sent him to us.

"Muhammad is not a father of any of you men, but the ambassador of God and the seal of all porphets, for God knows all things" (ch. 33, v. 40).

He is to be followed because as a child, as a youth, as a husband, as a father, as a ruler over men, and as a workman, as a trader, and as a servant of God, as the most loyal friend of his friends, and as a most merciful benefactor of his enemies, as a worshipper of Allah, and as a guide of the worshippers of Allah, as a custodian of the properties of the poor and the weak, as a most persevering and patient sufferer under the utmost cruelties of his fellow-men, as a rich man having authority over the treasures of a kingdom, and as a poor wanderer in search of God's light, as a judge and peacemaker and lover of all mankind without distinction he has set us an example the like of which is not to be found in the history of mankind.

" Surely, ye have most excellent exemplar in the ambassador of God for everyone who has faith in God and the Future Day and who remembers God much" (ch. 33, v. 21). And it is for this reason that the respect due to any monarch.

"O ye who believe ; raise not your voices above the voice of the Prophet and speak not to him in the rough way you speak to one another lest your deeds become void without your being aware.

"Surely those who lower their voices before the ambassador of God are those whose hearts God has proved for reverence ; for them is a forgiveness and a great reward" (ch 49, vv. 2, 3).

But with all this there never was a gentler and kinder heart than his, so gentle and so kind that his enemies taunt him with being womanish, for surely no mother ever born is so tender to her young ones as is this Ambassador of God to his fellow-men.

"What a mercy from God that thou (O Muhammad) art so gentle towards them and hadst thou been rough and hard of heart they would have dispersed from around thee." Muhammad is gentle, but God is most merciful, for the verse continues by God's command :—

"So, (O Muhammad) pardon thou them and ask forgiveness (from God) in their favour and consult them in the affair. But when thou hast made up thy mind then rely upon God, for God loves those who rely (Upon Him)" (ch. 3, v. 159).

Was there ever such a kind ambassador ? And so is Allah, who has prescribed mercy for Himself for those who seek it.

No man is ever anything but human, but out of His own grace God has made our hearts gentle and kind and He has made Muhammad (peace be upon him) the gentlest and most merciful of all men.

"Most surely an ambassador from amongst
yourselves has come to you, it is very hard on him
that you should be in distress; he is extremely
desirous for your good, and unto the believers
longing, merciful" (ch. 9, v. 128).

This Prophet, this Light of God, does not seek
any advantage for himself, because as to himself
God has promised him full satisfaction, and all his
dues have been paid up and his actions have been
fully rectified by God Almighty.

"Surely we have given thee (O Muhammad) a
clear decision so that Allah forgives thee all that is
due by thee or shall become due by thee and He
has completed His favour upon thee and guides thee
on the right path" (ch. 48, v. 1). This ambassador
does not draw any salary from us, his salary is with
his Lord.

"Say, I ask not from you salary for this work
and I am not one of those who are ostentatious.

"This (Quran) is a reminder unto all mankind.
And you will surely know all the news after a
while " (ch. 38, vv. 86, 87, 88).

"And we have not sent thee except as a bearer
of good news and as a warner unto all mankind
but most men know it not " (ch. 34, v. 28).

And once again God orders Muhammad to
proclaim :—

"Say, O ye men ! surely I am the ambassador of God towards you all whose is the kingdom of heavens and the earth ; there is no ruler but He, He gives life, He causes death. Then believe ye (all mankind) in God and His ambassador the unletter- ed prophet who believes in God and his word and follow him that you may be guided" (ch. 7, v. 158).

Do you see why this Light must be followed, this ambassador must be obeyed ? Because he comes from One to whom belongs the whole universe, who is Master over life and death. Muhammad (peace be upon him) is a man like the rest of us, but he is clothed with inspiration from God, with authority from One who is all powerful. And he comes to us for our good. We obey him for our own Salvation.

"Say : I am but a mortal like you, only it has been inspired unto me that your God is One God, hence, whoever in the service of his Lord" (ch. 18, v. 110).

Do you Gentlemen wish to meet your Lord ? Then follow His messenger for he will lead you to everlasting happiness. You have heard his last sermon delivered at Hajjatul-Balagh, you have heard the pledge he took from the converts of Madina at Akaba, near Mecca. He is calling you now. Obey him and be saved. Disobey him and you are responsible for your undoing. He has carried out his embassy.

"Whoever obey the ambassador surely obeys God, and whoever turns away from him, we have not sent thee (O Muhammad) a keeper over them" (ch. 4, v. 80).

And it is not only so with Muhammad (peace be on him), but has always been so with all the prophets.

"And we never sent a messenger but he was obeyed with the permission of God" (ch. 4, v. 64). Our God is one God and He is most merciful and ever inviting us through His messengers towards His mercy, and He has sent down Muhammad as the last great light in the firmament of Spirituality. He has purified him with His own Light and this Light is now purifying our hearts, may God bless him ever more and more and bless us also !

"O Ye who believe !
Remember God, remembering often.
And glorify Him morning and evening.
He sends His blessings on you
And so do His angels,
That He may bring you out of darkness
    into light,
For God is most merciful (in dealing) with
    the believers

Their salutation on the day they meet Him
Shall be "Peace"
For He has prepared for them
A most honourable reward
O thou prophet!
We have sent thee
As a witness
And a bringer of good news,
And as a warner,
And a caller unto God
With His permission
And a light-producing sun,
And give glad tidings to the believers
That for tnem is a great favour
From their Lord" (ch. 33 ,vv. 41-47).
And now I close my humble work with a
prayer :—

"All salutations, prayers and holy things
are due to God
Peace be on thee, O Prophet!
And the mercy of God
And His blessing,
Peace be upon us
And upon all virtuous servants of God ;
And bear witness that there is no one who
deserves to be worshipped except God,
And I bear witness that
Muhammad is His servant,
And ambassador." Amen.

# CHAPTER IV.

## What others say about the "Last Law Giver"

### NEPOLEAN BONAPART.

 PRAISE God and have great reverence for the Holy Prophet Muhammad and the Holy Quran.

### GEORGE BERNARD SHAW.

"I have always held the religion of Muhammad in the highest esteem because of its wonderful vitality. It is the only religion, which appears to me to possess that assimilating capability to the changing phases of existence which can make itself appeal to every age. The word much doubtless attach high value to the predictions of great men like me. I have prophesied about the faith of Muhammad that it would be acceptable to the Europe of tomorrow, as it is beginning to be acceptable to the Europe of to-day. The Medieval ecclesiastics, either through ignorance or bigotry, painted Muhammadanism in the darkest colours. They were in fact trained to hate the man Muhammad and his religion. To them Muhammad was

Anti-christ. I have studied him—the wonderful man and in my opinion, far from being an Anti-christ, he must be called the saviour of humanity. I believe that if a man like him were to assume the dictatorship of the modern world, he would succeed in solving its problems in a way that would bring it, the much needed peace and happiness.

## MAHATMA GANDHI'S TRIBUTE TO THE PROPHET.

" In its glorious days Islam was not intolerant. It commanded the admiration of the world. When the West was sunk in darkness, a bright star rose in the Eastern firmament and gave light and comfort to a groaning world. Islam is not a false religion. Let Hindus study it reverently and they will love it even as I do."

"I passed from the Companions to the Prophet himself. When I closed the second volume, I was sorry there was no more for me to read of that great life. I became more than ever convinced that it was not the sword that won a place for Islam in those days in the scheme of life. It was the rigid simplicity, the utter self-effacement of the Prophet, the scrupulous regard for pledges, his intense devotion to his friends and followers, his intrepidity, his fearlessness, his absolute trust in God and in his own mission. These and not the sword carried everything before them and surmounted every obstacle."

"Someone has said that Europeans in South Africa dread the advent of Islam—Islam that civilised Spain, Islam that took the torchlight to Morocco and preached to the world the Gospel of brotherhood. The Europeans of South Africa dread the advent of Islam, for they are afraid of the fact that if the native races embrace Islam they may claim equality with the white races. They may well dread it. If brotherhood is a sin, if it is equlity of the coloured races that they dread, then that dread is well founded. For I have seen that any Zulu embracing Christianity does not *ipso facto* come on a level with the Christians; whilst immediately he embraces Islam, he drinks from the same cup and eats from the same dish as a Mussalman. That is what they dread.

### H. E. SIR KISHEN PRASAD.

His Excellency Maharajah Sir Kishen Prasad Bahadur Yaminus Saltanat, K.C . I. E. G., C. I. E., President H. E. H. the Nizam's Executive Council, Hyderabad, Deccan.

My life I offer for Ahmad the Chosen one
Behold he is undoubtedly my Guide.

My humble person He did uplift to eminence.
Behold the glory of the Glorious God.

## THE GREAT BABA NANAK FOUNDER OF SIKHISM.

*By S. Piaras Singh.*

Guru Nanak, the great founder of Sikhism was a saint and sage of world-wide fame. He was born about five hundred years ago, at Nankana Sahib in Sheikhupura District in the Punjab  Though a born Hindu of the high-caste Bedi Khatri family, all along his life he professed a deep love for Islam and the Prophet of Islam

His passionate love for the Prophet took Guru Nanak all the way to Arabia. Twice he performed the Pilgrimage to Mecca and visited the Prophet's tomb at Madina.

He observed *chilas* (seclusion for divine contemplation) at Sirsa and Multan.  *Ya Allah* (O Allah) is still to be seen imprinted at Panja Sahib.  The copy of the Holy Quarn, from which the Guru would read out the divine message is still to be seen at Guru Har Sahai in Ferozepore District.  A picture drawn at the time of undertaking the *haj* is still preserved at Peshawar.  Even to this day, there is kept at Dera Baba Nanak, as a religious relic, that famous *chola* (shirt), which belonged to and was worn by Guru Nanak himself. As will be seen by the reduced facsimile illustration, the *chola* is profusely imprinted with Quranic verses, which shows but too plainly the nature and extent of that profound love and respect that the Guru had for Islam and the Holy Prophet.

The Great Guru's beautiful teachings breathe an out and out Islamic spirit. The Garanth Sahib is full of references to Islamic doctrines and the Prophet. Here are a few:—

"God is one. He is the Truth and the Truthful. He has created heavens and earth out of nothing. He is infinite, fearless and harmles. He is immortal. He is not born, nor is any one born of him. Ye is above resemblence to any one, nor is He capable of incarnation into any human form. He is *Rahman* (Beneficent) *Rahim* (Merciful) and Eeverlasting."

"The age for the Vedas and Puranas is gone: now the Quran is the only book to guide the world."

"The saints, reformers, martyrs, *Pirs*, Sheikhs and Qutubs will read untold benefit if they will send *Daruds* (God's blessings) on the Holy Prophet."

"The only reason as to why man is constantly restless and goes to hell is that he has no regard for the Prophet," (Peace and blessings of God be on him.)

## SADHU T. L. VASWANI.

**"A Hero Prophet.**—I salute Muhammad as one of the world's mighty heroes, Muhammad has been a world force, a mighty power for the uplift of many peoples. Read the old records, and you will glimps the grace and beauty of his life. A king and a spiritual leader, he yet mends his clothes. He hearkens to the call of the Unseen. "O thou enwrapped in thy mantle ! Arise and preach !" They persecute him ; his very life is in danger ; but he is loyal to the 'Call' ; he moves about preaching the way of peace. Muhammad was a hero and a prophet ; and I have often meditated on the last word whispered by him before he passed away : "Lord ; grant me pardon, and join me to the fellowship on high !" Who will not say that such a man was 'beautiful' in life, beautiful in death '?

And consider for a moment what the faith he preached has achieved. Islam has given the world a religion without priests. Islam abolished infanticide in Arabia ; Islam enjoined on the faithful total abstinence from drink, Islam emphasised the great qualities of faith, courage, endurance and self-sacrifice.

*A Puritanism.*—Islam introduced a vigorous puritanism into Asia and Europe, deprecating even
dancing and card playing. Who is Muslim, says
the Quran, he seeketh after the right way. Islam
moved out with its great message of Allah the
Rahman, the merciful, and became the torch bearer
of culture and civilisation in Africa, in China, in
Central Asia, in Europe, in Persia in India...... Of
the achievements of Islam in the days of the
Baghdad Khilafat every Muslim may be proud and
every Sindhi too : for Sindhis had their share in
the intellectual life of the Baghdad Court. Of the
achievements of Islam in Europe, less is known to
the Muslims and Hindus in Sindh ; yet even a rapid
sketch will show how much Islam did for Europe in
the Middle ages. Islam founded the great
University of Cordova which attracted Christian
scholars from different parts of Europe. One of these
scholars became, in due course, the Pope of Rome

*Muslims and Europe.*—At a time when Europe was
in darkness, the Muslim scholars of Spain held high
the torch of science and literature. They taught
medicine and mathematics, chemistry and natural
history, philosophy and fine arts. And it is no exag-
geration to say that Islam has made several contri-
butions to the thought and life of India. Islam
has been one of the nationalising forces in India.
Islam has enriched the art and architecture, the

goetry and philosophy of India. The Taj is perhaps the most imaginative architecture in the world."

## Mrs. SAROJINI NAIDU.

*Democracy and Brotherhood.*—It was the first religion that preached and practised democracy, for, in the mosque when the Minaret is sounded and the worshipers are gathered together, the democracy of Islam is embodied five times a day, when the peasant and the king kneel side by side and proclaim " God alone is great. " I have been struck over and, over again by this indivisible unity of Islam that makes a man instinctly a brother. When you meet an Egyptian, an Algerian, an Indian and Turk in London, what matters it that Egypt was the motherland of one and India the motherland of another ?

## Mr LALA LAJPAT RAI.

I have not the least hesitation in declaring that I entertain highest respect for the Prophet of Islam. In my opinion he holds the highest rank amongst Religious Teachers and Reformers.

## MAJOR ARTHUR GLYN LEONARD

( From " Islam, her Moral and Spiritual Value " )

*The Great Humanist*—In reality Muhammad was an ultra great man. The difference (as it appears to me) between other great men and himself was wide. The ordinary type of great man—a John Knox for example—is a patriot essentially. He is for his country first, then for God and humanity. As I have shown, with Muhammad it was just the reverse. An Arab by accident of birth he put God and nature before everything It was this that made him a humanist, this that placed him before his age For Muhammad without a shadow of doubt was centuries before his age

*The Great Constructor* —A man not only great, but one of the greatest—*i. e*, truest-men that Humanity has ever produced. Great, *i. e.*, not simply as a prophet but as a patriot and a states-man : a material as well as a spiritual builder who constructed a great nation, a greater empire, and more even than all these, a still greater Faith· True, moreover, because he was true to himself, to his people, and above all to his God.

The man of fixed and unchanging purpose has a supreme contempt for obstacles. But when, as in Muhammad's case that purpose is the glorification of God, he has at hand a lever that can move the world In this peculiar sense the great Prophet of Arabia was self-contained. He has everything within himself : that everything centred in God and Arabian unity. He sought only what he needed

This was to unify God and his country. How he succeeded is a matter of history.

Muhammad was a thinker and a worker, not only for his own, but for all times. He recognised that man was equally a political and religious product of God's creation. He understands that as a counterpoise to man's materialism and to the destructive in his nature, is that indefinable essence which we call the spirit and the constructive.

*Muhammad's Devoutness and Righteousness* —To Muhammad in ever vibrating star an all-seeing eye and glory of the great Creator, God was visible, in every tiny blade of grass, n every spring of water He was manifest and tangible  . . . .

A more devout man than Muhammad never lived. He was as pre-eminently wise as he was devout. He utilised his wisdom to the fullest extent of his capacity, and he proved his devoutness by putting his beliefs to the infallible test of stern and rigid practice. A trade to his finger tips, a clearsighted man of business, and a statesman with prophetic instincts. 'Who profited by the past utilised the present, and prepared for the future . .  . Dutiful and obedient to his uncle who had been a father to him, he was a faithful servant and exemplary husband, a kind father and a good master. The very name of faithful, (*amin*) by which he was always distinguished, proves beyond doubt what manner of man he was .. ..... . .... ... ... ....

.........In this righteous sense Muhammad was curious. As one of her own selection, nature had specially endowed him with curiosity. He was one of her human, sensitive plants. As an observer, all his senses were developed and on the alert. He not only saw, but felt every vibration that thrilled, as it were, the very soul of the first great mother. In every fleeting cloud, as in every fugitive thought, he was conscious of an unseen Power. A look-out man rather than a prophet, it was thus he groped or rather felt his way until he felt God.

*A Creed of Practice.*—Muhammad's sincerity and fixity of purpose is a fact we cannot get away from. It is this with which he chained his followers as with the sure cord of God to the faith. Islam, in a word, is a creed of practice not theory. By practice it was formed. On practice it has lived. It was because Muhammad practised what he preached, that the small seed of his original idea blossomed at last into the might "Igdrasil" of the East.. . .the great banyan tree of existence.

*The Soul of Islam is the spirit of Muhammad.*—In his God-concept, in his rejection of the ancient myth of immaculate conception, in his refusing to acknowledge Christ's Divinity, he was essentially a modern—a modern of the 20th century. It was this Catholicity therefore that made Islam blossom into a spiritual energy that embraces so many national units. Muhammad fought with all his might and main. In exact proportion to his labour he has prevailed, prevailed over the issues of life and death Death had no terror for him. Life alone was full of terror, i. e., of the fear of God. In death there was no sting. In grave there was no victory. Death but filled the mortal part of him. The spiritual it has increased and multiplied out of all proportion. The present soul of Islam is the spirit of Muhammad. Only when this exhausts itself will Islam wither and die ! To this day he is, and for many æons to come he will be in spirit, the ruler and judge over Islam. Inspite of sects and theological speculators, as long as Islam lasts, his spirit will continue to preside over its destinies. His spirit lives in the spirit of the creed that he bequeathed as a divine legacy to humanity, i. e., to those sections of it which have been nurtured in the system and adoration of the Patriach. For though the material part of him is dead, the spiritual still speaks with a voice that is myriad-tongued.

*The Great Genius.*—If genius implies a keen psychological insights into the nature and inner consciousness of life's issue, added to inexhaustible energy, capacity for work and patience, then Muhammad was a genius. Certainly if we accept Buffons' definition of genius, as, "but a greater aptitude for perseverance" he was without doubt a genius of the highest degree. The founder of a faith —one of the greatest the world has produced— spiritual commander of the faithful, his genius was essentially moral and religious. His whole life was one long labour of love and devotion to achieve his object, *i. e.* to proclaim God to the nations of the earth.

*His Faith in God.*—His centre of gravity was God. This gravity formed his character, gave him courage and endurance in all his trials and afflictions, counselled and guided him in his ordinary vocations. It was this gravity and concentration that commanded the respect and trust of all who knew him and came under his magnetic influence ...... ..With him, "life was but a means to an end, that end, beginning, means and end to all things—God."

*The Arabs and Civilisation.*—Do not we, who now consider ourselves on the topmost pinnacle ever reached by culture and civilization. recognise that had it not been for the high culture, and civilisation and intellectual as well as soci  splendour of Arabs, and to the soundness of their school

system. Europe to this day has remained sunk in
the darkness of ignorance! Have we forgotten that
the Muhammadan maxim was that, " the real
learning of a man if of more public importance than
any particular religious opinion he may entertain"
—that Muslim liberty was in striking contrast with
the then intolerant state of Europe.

*Muslim Scholars* —It is possible that Europe is
unmindful of, and has the ingratitude to ignore, the
splendid services of the scientists and philosophers
of Arabia ? Are the names of 'Assamh, Abu Oth-
man, Alberuni, Albeithar, Abu Ali Ibn Sina (Avi-
cenna), the great physician and philosopher, Ibn
Rushad (Averroes) of Cordova the chief commenta-
tor on Aristotle, Ibn Bajja (Avenlace) besides a
host of others, but dead letters ? Is the great work
that they have done and the fame that they have
left behind them in their books, to be consigned
to the limbo of oblivion, by an ungrateful because antipathetic Europe ? Does the work of
Alhezen, author of optical treatises who understood
the weight of air, corrected the Greek misconcep-
tion of theory of vision, and determined the
function of Retina, count for nothing ? Do we
owe no tribute to a great thinker such as Ghazali,
who in speaking of his attempts to detach himself
from his youthful opinions says : " I said to myself
my aim is simply to know the truth of things,

consequently it is indispensable for me to ascertain what is knowledge "?

With experience and facts such as these before me, I for one find it impossible to forget. and only natural to acknowledge with candour, the great and magnificent part that Islam has occupied in the history of the world. In the intellectual strife of heroes who have wrestled and fought for the truth and who for many centruies led the world, in the arena of battle and of conquest, where warriors have led the van, the sons of Islam stand on a pedestal of their own making, that as the world grows older and more enlightened, will stand out in all the reater prominence.

### Rev BOSSWORTH SMITH

[ From " Lectures on Muhammad and Muhammadanism" ]

*Islam Dignifies the Humble.*—Christian Travellers, with every wish to think otherwise have remarked that the Negro who accepts Muhammadanism acquires at once a sense of dignity of human nature not commonly found even among those who have been brought to accept Christianity.

Here then we find in Central Africa the use of decent clothing, and the arts of reading and agriculture, attributed to Islam.

*The Estimate of the value of Islam.*—A religion which indisputably has made cannibalism and human sacrifice impossible, which has introduced reading and writing, and, what is more, which has introduced love for them ; which has forbidden, and, to a great extent, has abolished, immodest dancing and gambling and drinking, which inculcated upon the whole a pure morality, and sets forth a sublime and at the same time a simple theology is surely deserving of other feelings than the hatred and the contempt which some portions of our religious press habitually pour upon it.

Truly, if the question must be put, whether it is Muhammadan or Christian nations that have as yet have done most for Africa, the answer must be that it is not the Christian. And if it be asked, again, now what religion is the purest in itself, and ideally the best, for this there could be but one answer : but which under the peculiar circumstances Historical, Geographical, and Ethnological, is the religion most likely to hold on a vast scale of the native mind and so in some measure to elevate the savage character, the same answer must be returned.

*The Work of Muhammad.*—By thus absolutely prohibiting gambling and intoxicating liquors, Muhammad did much to abolish, once for all, over the vast regions that own his away, two of the vast and most irremediable evils of European society; evils to the intensity of which Christian governments of the Nineteenth Century are hardly yet beginning to awake.

*A True Friend.*——If the warmth of the attachment may be measured, as in fact it may, by the depth of his friends' devotion to him, no true friend than Muhammad ever lived. Around him in quite early days, gathered what was best and noblest in Mecca; and in no single instance, through all the vicissitudes of his checquered life, was the friendship then formed ever broken. The most note-worthy of his external characteristics were a sweet gravity and a quite dignity, which drew involuntary respect, and which was the best and often the only protection which he enjoyed from insult.

*Vitality of Islam*——It is that religion which alone gives stability to the tottering fabric, and is the one piinciple of life amidst all the jarring elements of destruction. It is the religion which merges all colours, ranks, and races in the consciousness of one brotherhood. It is the religion which elevates the minds by drawing from the Transitory to the Eternal, and which gives to half-starved or ill-used peasant that courage in calamity, that calm amidst confusion, and that ineffable dignity in distress, which is found nowhere but in Islam.

*Muhammad Ruled Human Heart.*—Head of the State as well of the Church, he was Caesar and Pope in one, but he was Pope without the Pope's pretensions, and Caesar without the legion of Caesar, without a standing army, without a body guard without a place, without a fixed revenue. If ever any man had the right to say that he ruled by a right divine, it was Muhammad, for he had all power without its instruments, and without its supports. He was superior to the titles and ceremonies, the solemn trifling, and the proud humility of the court etiquette. To hereditary kings, to princes born in the purple these things are, naturally enough, as the breath of life, but those ought to have known better even self-made rulers, and those the foremost in the files of time—a Caesar, a Cromwell, a Napoleon, —have been unable to resist their tinsel attraction Muhammad was content with the reality, he cared not for the dressings of power. The simplicity of his private life was in keeping with his public life.

*Muhammad's Miracle.*—By a fortune absolutely unique in history, Muhammad is a threefold founder—' of a nation, of an empire, and of a religion ' Illiterate himself, scarcely able to read or write he was yet the author of a book which is a poem, a code of laws, a Book of common Prayer and a Bible in one, and is reverenced to this day by a sixth of the whole human race as a miracle of purity of style, of wisdom and of truth. It was the one miracle, claimed by Muhammad—' his standing miracle' he called it, and miracle indeed it is. But looking at the circumstances of the time, at the unbounded reverence of his followers, and comparing him with the Fathers of the Church, or with mediaeval saints, to my mind the most miraculous thing about Muhammad is, that he never claimed the power of working miracles. Whatever he had said, he could do, his disciples would straight away have seen him do. They could not help attributing to him miraculous acts, which he never did, and which he always denied he could do. What more crowning proof of his sincerity is needed? Muhammad to the end of his life claimed for himself that title only with which he had begun, and which the highest philosophy and the truest Christianity will one day, I venture to believe, agree in yielding to him—that of a Prophet, a very Prophet of God.

### Rev. JOHN DEVENPORT

[From "Apology for Quran and Muhammad"]

*And Ideal Personality.*—His politeness to the great, his affabiltiy to the humble, and his dignified bearing to the presumptuous, procured him respect, admiration and applause His talents were equaly

fitted for persuasion or command. Deeply read in
the volume of nature, though entirely ignorant of
letters, his mind could expand in controversy with
the acutest of his enemies, or contract itself to the
apprehensions of the meanest of his disciples. His
simple eloquence, rendered impressive by the expression of a countenance, wherein awfulness of
majesty was tempared by an amiable sweetness,
excited emotions of veneration and love ; and he was
gifted with the authoritative air of genius which
alike influences the learned and commands the
illiterate. As a friend and a parent he exhibited
the softest feelings of our nature ; but, while in
possession of the kind and generous emotions of the
heart and engaged in the discharge of most of the
social and domestic duties, he disgraced not his assumed title of an apostle of God. With all that
simplicity which is natural to a great mind he performed the humbler offices whose homeliness it
would be idle to conceal with pompous diction ; even
while Lord of Arabia, he mended his own shoes and
coarse woollen garments, milked the ewes, swept
the hearth, and kindled the fire. Dates and water
were his usual fare and milk and honey his luxuries.
When he travelled he divided his morsel with his
servant. The sincerity of his exhortation to
benevolence was justified at his death by the exhausted state of his coffers.

*His Earnestness and Sincerity.*—The view taken
by Thomas Carlyle of this hero-Prophet is too
original, just and striking to be here omitted :—
"The deep-hearted son of the wilderness" writes he,
"with his beaming black eyes, and open social deep
soul, had other thoughts in him than ambition. A
silent, great soul, he was one of those who cannot
but be earnest, whom Nature herself had appointed
to be sincere. While others walk in formulas and
hearsays, contented enough to dwell therein, this
man could not screen himself in formulas; he was
alone with his own soul and the reality of things.
The great mystery of existence glared in upon him,
with its terrors, with its splendours; no hearsays
could hide that unspeakable fact, 'Hear am I !'.
Such sincerity as we named, it has, in truth, something of divine. The word of such a man is a voice
direct from Nature's own heart. Men do and must
listen to that, or to nothing else,—all else is wind in
comparison. From of old a thousand thoughts in
his pilgrimages and wanderings had been in this
man, 'What am I? What is the unfathomable
Thing I live in, which men name Universe? What
is Life? What is Death?' What am I to believe?
What am I to do?' The grim rocks of Mount Hara,
of Mount Sinai, the stern solitudes answered not.
The great heaven rolling silently overhead with its
blue glancing stars, answered not. There was no

answer. The man's own soul, and what of God's
inspiration dwelt therein, had to answer "

*The service of Mankind a Criterion of Righteousness*.
"It is not righteousness that ye turn your face
towards the east or the west but righteousness is
(in) him who believeth in God and the Last day,
and the angles and the Scripture and the prophets
and who giveth wealth for the love of God to kins-
folk and to orphans and the needy and the son of the
road, and those who are constant in prayer and
giveth the alms, and those who fulfil their covenants
whent hey covenant, and the patient in adversity
and affliction and in time of violence, these are they
who are true and these are they who fear God."

*Muhammad and Warfare.*—The messenger sent
by Muhammad to Governor of Bossa, near Damascus
was taken prisoner and murdered by Sherheil, an
Emir of a Christian and Arabian tributary to
Heraclius, the Greek Emperor. Three thousand
men were equipped to fight with the Greek in the
cause of Allah the Most High and Muhammad
preached to them: "In avenging my injuries,
molest not the harmless votaries of domestic
seolusion; spare the weakness of the softer sex, the
infant at the breast, and those who, in the course of
nature, are hastening from the scene of mortality.
Abstain from demolishing the dwellings of the

unresisting inhabitants and destoiy not the means of subsistence; respect their fruit trees nor injure the plam, so useful to Syria for its shade and so delightful for its verdure."

*A Prophet and Nation Builder.*—Muhammad, a private man, made himself to be looked upon as a prophet of his own family. Muhammad, a simple Arab, united the distracted, scanty, naked and hungry tribes of his country into one compact and obedient body and presented them with new attributes and a new character among the peoples of the earth. In less than thirty years this system defeated the Emperor of Constantinople, overthrew the Kings of Persia : subdued Syria, Mesopotamia, Egypt; and extended its conquests from Atlantic to the Caspian ocean and to the Oxus ; from which limits during twelve centuries, its political sway has never, with the exception of Spain only, receded; while the faith has continued to extend, and is, at this hour, extending in Northern Asia, in Central Africa, and on the Caspian.

Such was Muhammad, the hero-prophet, whose enthusiasm and genius founded a religion which was to reduce the followers of Zoroaster to a few scattered communities, to invade India, to over power the ancient Brahamanism, as well as the more widespread Buddhism even beyond the Ganges ; to wrest her most ancient and venerable provinces from Christianity, to subjugate by Degress the whole of her Eastern Dominions and Roman Africa, from Egypt to the straits of Gibraltar, to assail Europe at its Western extremity, to possess the greater part of Spain, and to advance to the borders of Loire, which was to make the Elder Rome tremble for her security, and, finally, to establish itself in triumph, with the new Rome of Constantinople

*His Son's Death.*—On the death of his only son, Ibrahim, .. .an eclipse of the sun occurred at the very hour of the youth's decease. The common people saw in this prodigy a sure token that the heavens themselves, shared the general grief, but so far from encouraging this superstitious feeling on the part of his ignorant followers, so far from listening to the voice of flattery. Muhammad called the people together and said to them: "Fellow-citizens, the sun and the stars are the works of God's hands, but they are neither eclipsed nor effaced to announce the birth or the death of mortals."

*Irresistible Charm of Koran.*—In a literary point of view the Koran is the most poetical work of the East. It is, confessedly, the standard of the Arabian language, and abounds with splendid imagery and the boldest metaphors, and not withstanding that it is sometimes obscure and verging upon timidity, is generally vigorous and sublime, so as to justify the observation of the celebrated Goethe, that the Koran is a work with whose dullness the reader is at first disgusted, afterwards attracted by its charms, and finally, irresistibly ravished by its many beauties.

*The Arabs as World Teachers.*—The first revivers of philosophy and the sciences, the link, as they have been termed, between ancient and modern literature, were, most undoubtedly, according to every species of testimony, the Saracens of Asia and the Moors of Spain under the Abbaside and the Ommaide caliphs.

"According to the unanimous accounts," says Mosheim, "of the most credible witnesses nothing could be more melancholy and deplorable than the darkness that reigned in the Western world during this (tenth) century which, with respect to learning and philosophy at least, may be called the Iron age of the Latins........ The philosophy of the Latins extended no further than the single science of Logic or dialectics, which they looked upon as the sum and substance of all human wisdom. It is certain that Arabian philosophers had already founded numerous schools in Spain and Italy, whither numbers of enquirers after knowledge repaired and having adopted the Arabian philosophical tenets and systems introduced them into the Christian Schools. And again, "It must be owned that all the knowledge, whether of physics,

astronomy, philosophy, or mathematics which
flourished in Europe from the 10th century, was
originally derived from the Arabian schools, and the
Spanish Saracen, in a more particular manner
may be looked upon as the father of European
philosophy." To the Arabs, modern Europe is
indebted for its first bud of poetic imagination
and of its visions of romance.

*The Muslims in Spain.*—Who has not mourn-
ed over the fate of the last remnant of chivalry,
the fall of the Mussalman Empire in Spain?
Who has not felt his bosom swell with
admiration towards that brave and generous nation
of whose reign of eight centuries, it is observed
even by the historians of their enemies that not
a single instance of cold-blooded cruelty is re-
corded? Who has not blushed to see Christian
priesthood goading on the civil power to treat
with unexampled bigotry and devilish cruelty, a
people from whom they had always received
humanity and protection; and to record the
political fanaticism of Ziemenes in consigning to
the flames the labours of the philosophers, mathe-
maticians and poets of Cordova, the literature of
a splendid dynasty of seven hundred years.

## SIR THOMAS CARLYLE

[ From " Hero and Hero-worship " ]

1. *The Character of Muhammad* —Muhammad
had no school learning ; of the thing we call school
learning none at all ..It seems to be the true
opinion that Muhammad could never write ... But,
from an early age, he had been remarked as a
thoughtful man, His companions named him Alam-
in, " The Faithful ". A man of truth and fidelity,
true in what he did, in what he spake and thought.
They noted that he always meant something A
man rather taciturn in speech . silent when there
was nothing to be said , but pertinent, wise, sincere
when he did speak , always throwing light on the
matter. This is the only sort of speech worth speaking. Through life we find him to have been regarded as an altogether solid, brotherly, genuine man.
A serious sincere character, yet amiable, cordial,
and companionable, jocose even.

2. *His Simplicity* —His household was of the
frugalest ; his common diet barley, bread and water,
sometimes for months there was not fire once light-
ed on his hearth They record with just pride that
he would mend his own shoes, patch his own cloak.
A poor, hard toiling, ill provided, man careless of
what vulgar men toil for. Not a bad man, I should
say ; something better in him than hunger of any

sort,—or these wild Arab men, fighting and jostling
three-and-twenty years at his hands, in close contact with him always would not have reverenced
him so! They were wild men, bursting ever and
anon into quarrel, into all kinds of fierce sincerity ;
without right worth and man-hood, no man could
have commanded them. They called him Prophet,
you, say? why, he stood there, face to face with
them ; bare, not enshrined in any mystery , visibly
clouting his own cloak, cobbling his own shoes,
fighting, counselling, ordering in the midst of
them ; they must have seen what kind of a man he
was, let him be called what you like! No emperor
with his tiaras was obeyed as this man in a cloak of
his own clouting. During three and twenty years
of rough actual trial, I find something of a verit-
able Hero necessary for that, of itself.

3. *The Coming of Light and Glory.*—To the
Arab Nation it was as a birth from darkness into
light; Arabia first became alive by means of it. A
poor shepherd people, roaming unnoticed in its
deserts since the creation of the world; a Hero
Prophet was sent down to them with a word they
could believe; see, the unnoticed becomes the
world notable, the small has grown the world-great,
within one centuary afterwards Arabia is at
Grenada on this hand, at Delhi on that , glancing in
valour and splendour and the light of genius, Arabia
shines through long ages over a great section of

the world.  Belief is great, life-giving.  The history of a nation becomes fruitful, soul-elevating, great, so soon as it believes.  These Arabs, the man Mahomet, and that one century,—is it not as if a spark had fallen, one spark, on a world of what seemed black un-noticeable sand , but lo, the sand proves explosive powder, blazes heaven-high from Delhi to Grenada ! I said , the great man was always as lightening out of Heaven , the rest of men waited for him like fuel, and then they too would flame ''

4.  *The Sincerity of Quran* —Sincerity, in all senses, seems to me the merit of the Quran , what had rendered it precious to the wild Arab men.  It is, after all, the first and the last merit in a book ; gives rise to merits of all kinds,—Nay, at bottom, it alone can give rise to merit of any kind.

### BY SIR WILLIAM MUIR.

[From " Life of Mahomet " ]

*Proof of the Sincerity of Muhammad.*—I will merely add that the simplicity and earnestness of Abu Bakr, and of Omar also, the first two Caliphs, are strong evidence of their belief in the sincerity of Mahomet ; and the belief of these men must carry undeniable weight in the formation of our own estimate of his character, since the

apportunities they enjoyed for testing the grounds
of their conviction were both close and long
continued. 'It is enough that I allude to this
consideration, as strengthening generally the view
of Mahomet's character which throughout I have
sought to support.'

*Muhammad's Treatment with His Life-long
Eenemies.*—In the exercise of a power absolutely
dictatorial, Mahomet was just and temperate.
Nor was he wanting in moderation towards his
enemies when once they had cheerfully submitted
to his claims. The long and obstinate struggle
against his pretensions maintained by the inhabitants of Mecca might have induced its conqueror
to mark his indignation in indelible traces of fire
and blood. But Mahomet, excepting a few crimi-
nals, granted a universal pardon; and nobly
casting into oblivion the memory of the past,
with all its mockery, its effronts and persecution,
he treated even the foremost of his opponents
with a gracious and even friendly consideration.
Not less marked was the forbearance shown to
Abdullah and the disaflected citizens of Madina,
who for many years persistently thwarted his
designs and resisted his authority, nor the cle-
mency with which he received the submissive
advances of tribes that before had been the most
hostile, even in the hour of victory.

*Muhammad Unparalleled in History.*—We search
in vain through the pages of profane history for a
parallel to the struggle in which for thirteen years
the Prophet of Arabia, in the face of discourage-
ment and threats, rejection and persecution, re-
tained thus his faith unwavering, preached repen-
tance, and denounced God's wrath against his
godless fellow citizens. Surrounded by a little
band of faithful men and women, he met insults,
menace, and danger with a lofty and patient trust
in the future. And when at last the promise of
safety came from a distant quarter he calmly
waited until his followers had all departed, and
then disappeared from amongst an ungrateful and
rebellious people.

*Benefits of Islam.*—And what have been the
effects of the system which, established by such
instrumentality, Mahomet has left behind him? We
may freely concede that it banished for ever many
of the darker elements of superstition for ages
shrouding the Peninsula. Idolatry vanished before
the battle cry of Islam ; the doctrine of the Unity
and infinite perfections of God, and of a special all
pervading Providence, became a living principle in
the hearts and lives of the followers of Mahomet,
even as in his own. An absolute surrender and
submission to the Divine Will (the idea embodied
in the very name of Islam) was demanded as the

first requirement of the faith. Nor are social virtues wanting. Brotherly love is inculcated towards all within the circle of the faith; infanticide proscribed; orphans to be protected; and slaves treated with consideration; intoxicating drinks prohibited, so that Mahometanism may boast of a degree of temperance unknown to any other creed.

## RICHARD POCOCKE BISHOP OF MEATH

[ From a " Description of the East and Other Countries, Vol I " ]

*Tolerant Character of Muhammad.*—(Proved by a document which is a patent of the Holy Prophet granted to the monks of Mount Sinai and Christians in general) :—

As God is great and governeth, from whom all the prophets are come, for there remaineth no record of injustice against God ; through the gifts that are given unto men Muhammad, the son of Abdullah, the Apostle of God, and careful guardian of the whole world, has written the present instrument, to all those that are his national people, and of his relig_ ion, as a secure and positive promise to be accomplish- ed to the Christian Nation and relations of the Naza- reen whosoever they may be, whether be noble or the vulgar, the honourable or otherwise, saying thus :

1. Whosoever of my nation shall presume to break my promise and oath which is contained in

this present agreement, destroys the promise of God acts contrary to the oath and will be a resister of the faith (which God forbid !) for he becometh worthy of the curse, whether he be the king himself or a poor man, or what person soever he may be.

2. That whenever any of the monks in his travels shall happen to settle on any mountain, hill, or village, or in any other habitable plaçe on the sea or in desert, or in any convent, church or house of prayer, I shall be in the midst of them, as the preserver and protector of them, their goods and effects, with my soul, aid and protection, jointly with all my national people, because they are a part of my people, and an honour to me.

3. Moreover, I command all officers not to require any poll-tax of them or any other tribute, because they shall not be forced or compelled to any thing of this kind.

4. None shall presume to change their Judges or Governors, but they shall remain in their office without being deposed.

5. No one shall molest them when they are travelling on the road.

6. Whatever churches they are possessed of, no one is to deprive them of them.

7. Whosoever shall annul any of these my decrees, let him know positively that he annuls the ordinance of God.

8. Moreover, neither their judges, governors, monks, servants, disciples, or any other depending on them, shall pay any poll-tax or be molested on that accounts, because I am their protector, whereso-ever they shall be, either by land or sea, east or west, north or south, because both they and all that belong to them are included in my promissory oath and patent.

9. And of those that live quietly and solitary upon the mountains, they shall exact neither poll-tax nor tithes from their incomes, neither shall any Mussalman partake of what they have, for they labour only to maintain themselves.

10. Whenever the crop of the earth shall be plentiful in its due time, the inhabitants shall be obliged, out of every bushal, to give them a certain measure.

11. Neither in time of war shall they take them out of their habitation, nor compel them to go to the wars, nor even then shall they require of them poll-tax.

12. Those Christians who are inhabitants and with there riches and traffic are able to pay the poll-tax, shall pay no more than 12 Darchms.

13. Excepting this, nothing more shall be required of them, according to the express word of God, that says, "Do not molest those that have a veneration for the Books that are sent from God, but rather, in a kind manner, give of your good things to them and converse with them, and hinder everyone from molesting them.

14. If a Christian woman shall happen to marry a Mussulman, the Mussulman shall not cross the inclination of his wife to keep her from her chapel and prayers and the practice of her religion.

15. That no person hinder them from repairing their churches.

16. Whosoever acts contrary to this my grant, or gives credit to anything contrary to it, becomes truly an apostate from God and his divine Apostle, because this protection I have granted to them according to this promise.

17. No one shall bear arms against them, but on the contrary. the Mussulmans shall wage war for them.

18. And by this I ordain that none of my nation shall presume to do or act contrary to this promise until the end of the world.

(Signed by 16 witnesses).

Written the 3rd of Moharam 2nd Hegira.

## PROF. T. W. ARNOLD.

[From " The Preaching of Islam " ]

*Islam and Priesthood.*—There being no inter-
mediary between the Muslim and his God, the
responsibility of his personal salvation rests upon
himself alone, consequently he becomes as a rule
much more strict and careful in the performance of
his religious duties, he takes more trouble to learn
the doctrines and observances of his faith and thus
becoming deeply impressed with the importance of
them to himself, is more likely to become an ex-
ponent of the missionary character of his creed in
the presence of unbeliever.

*A Missionary Religion.*—It is such a zeal for the
truth of their religion that has inspired the Mohem-
madans to carry with them the Message of Islam to
the people of every land into which they penetrate,
and that justly claims for their religion a place
among those we term missionary.........

Further, the vast and unparalleled success of
the Muslim arms shook the faith of the Christian
people that came under their rule and saw in their
conquests the hand of God, worldly prosperity they
associated with the divine favour, and the God of
battle (they thought) would surely give the victory
only into the hands of his favoured servants. Thus
the very success of the Mohammadans seemed to

argue the truth of their religion ...Even Muslim prisoners will on occasions embrace the opportunity of preaching his faith to his captors or to his fellow prisoners. The 1st introduction of Islam into Eastern Europe was the work of a Muslim Juris-consult who was taken prisoner....... .He set before many of them the teaching of Islam and they embraced the faith with sincerity, so that it began to spread among this people.

*The Universal Brotherhood.*—But above all—and herein is its supreme importance in the missionary history of Islam—it ordains a yearly gathering of believers of all nations and languages, brought together from all parts of the world, to pray in that sacred place towards which their faces are set in every hour of private worship in their distant homes. No stretch of religious genius could have conceived a better expedient for impressing on the minds of the faithful a sense of their common life and of their brotherhood in the bonds of faith. Here in a supreme act of common worship the Negro of the West coast of Africa meets the Chinaman from the distant east; the courtly and polished Ottoman recognises his brother Muslim in the wild islander from the farthest end of Malayan Sea. At the same time throughout the whole Muhammadan world the hearts of believers are lifted up in sympathy with their more fortunate brethern gathered together in the sacred city, as in their own homes they celebrate the festival of Id-ul-Adha or the feast of Bayram (as it is called in Turkey and Egypt). Their visit to the sacred city has been to many Muslims the experience that has stirred them up to strive in the path of God.

*Muslim Spain* —Muslim Spain has written one of the brightest pages in the history of a mediaeval Europe. She had inaugurated the age of chivalry and her influence had passed through Provence into the other countries of Europe, bringing into birth a new poetry and a new culture, and it was from her that the Christian scholars received what of Greek Philosophy and Science they had to simulate their mental activity up to the time of the Renaissance.

### PROF. E. MONET OF FRANCE

[ A Quotation from Arnold ]

*Islam a Rationalism.*—Islam is a religion that is essentially rationalistic in the widest sense of the term considered etymologically and historically. The definition of rationalism as a system that bases religious beliefs on principles furnished by the reason, applies to it exactly. It is ture that Muhammad, who was an enthusiast and possessed too, the ardour of faith and fire of conviction—that precious quality he transmitted to so many of his disciples—brought forward his reform as a revelation, but this kind of revelation is only one form of exposition and his religion has all the masks of a bundle of doctrines founded on the data of reason. ..... .A creed so precise, so stripped of all theological complexities and consequently so accessible to the ordinary understanding, might be expected to possess and does indeed possess a marvellous power of winning its way into the consciences of men

## STANELY LANEPOOLE

[ From "Speeches and Table-talks of Muhammad " ]

*A Mercy to Mankind.*—He was gifted with mighty powers of imagination, elevation of mind, delicacy and refinement of feeling. "He is more modest than a virgin behind her curtain," it is said of him. He was most indulgent to his inferiors, and would never allow his awkward little page to be scolded whatever he did. "Ten years," said Anas, his servant, "was I about the prophet and he never said as much as 'uff' to me." He was very affectionate towards his family; He was very fond of children, he would stop them in the streets and pat their little heads. He never struck any one in his life. The worst expression he ever made use of in conversation was "What has come to him ? May his forehead be darkened with mud." When asked to curse some one he replied,

" I have not been sent to curse, but to be a mercy to
mankind." He visited the sick, followed any bier
he met, accepted the invitation of a slave to dinner,
mended his own clothes, milked the goats, and
waited upon himself, relates summarily another tradition. He never first withdrew his hand out of
another man's palm, and turned not before the other
man had turned.

"He was the most faithful protector of those
he protected, the sweetest and most agreeable in
conversation. Those who saw him were suddenly
filled with reverence; those who came near him
loved him; they who described him would say,
'I have never seen his like either before or after.
He was of great taciturnity, but when he spoke it
was with emphasis and deliberation and no one
could forget what he said."

### Dr. JULIUS GERMANUS, OF HUNGARY

[ From a lecture delivered by him in Lahore in December, 1930 ]

*The Most Perceptive Religion.*—Islam in its
glorious march has connected millions of people
who lived in quite different regions, and quite
different social and economical environments that
the Arabs among whom the Prophet first preached
the Quran. Islam has proved the most perceptive
religion, as in its onward march—retaining and

strictly clinging to the ethic fundamentals of the
revelation—has amalgamated in itself all the
requirements of the times in order to serve the
spiritual needs of its adherents. We may boldly
say that God has not created mankind for Islam,
but He revealed Islam to serve the moral and
spiritual needs of its believers.

*Muslims and Learning.*—We may safely say, that
Islam, its force and extensive power, has contributed
to a self-awakening of Europe from its lethargy
and shaped it into a steady spiritual power. So,
while Islam and Christianity stood as two hostile
bodies against one another, Christian spiritual
culture and even political organisation was influenced and moulded by Islam. There was a time when
learning in Europe could be derived only through
the medium of the Arabic tongue, which was the
language of Islam, and European scholars went to
Spain to enrich their minds with the treasures of
knowledge, amassed in its schools and libraries.
Arts and crafts flourished in Islamic countries to
such a perfection, town life developed to such a
height that when the industrious Arabs were driven
out of Spain, manufacturing skill suddenly relapsed
in Spain in the XVI Century. These things are too
well known to need arguments, but they must be
mentioned to put down for ever the assumption
that Islam could not create a culture. Nothing is

more absurd. Islam has brought forth tremendous armies which in equipment, strategy and discipline surpassed the armies of the then inhabited world; it created and preserved a learning and advanced science from which all European nations have learned.

*Priesthood No More.*—Muhammad the Prophet had broken the spell of priesthood beforelong; Islam did not need a mediator between God and man. It was a democratic religion from the beginning. No institution stood between the Creator and created. Through the knowledge of the Quran every body had access to the revelation, which would be expounded freely, without any synod putting limitations upon it. In this respect Islam did not need a reformation similar to that in Christianity, and as a matter of fact the democratic spirit which has reigned in Islam, began in Christianity only with the rise of nationalism and the Reformation.

## MAJOR-GENERAL FORLONG

[ From "Short Studies in the Science of Comparative Religions " ]

*The Virtuous Prophet.*—After long, very full and candid study of the great Arabian and his faith, his public and private character, virtues and defects; his times and circumstances—a study extending over forty years and in close connection with

Muhammadans of all sets and nations, we must confess that the Prophet stands high in the list of the greatest of the earth's rulers and the makers of history. Alike in camp and Council, as a governor of men, administrator and organiser of brave and turbulent tribes or settled nations. Muhammad commanded the respect of statesmen, friends and foes; and was loved, honoured and esteemed by all privileged to know him privately or publicly.

*Muslim Ruler's Love for Learning.*—As soon as its rule was firmly established in Western Asia, Africa and Southern Europe, its rulers did their best to upraise the people intellectually. It was they, says the author of the 'History of European Civilization' who kindled the lamp of learning which illumined the dark pages of European History; which but for the Arabs might never have become a centre of civilization and progress." They established seats of learning from Spain to Baghdad. There teachers and scholars arose—bright and shining lights—the cultured saviours of Europe when Christians were ignorant gloomy. pessimists. busy only in darkening the land with all the devout senility which characterised our dark middle ages.

*Muslims and Polygamy*—Muhammadans "look upon polygamy as a remedy of many social evils and they are not far wrong," says Max Muller. In all that concerns that great leader we must remember the land, circumstances and ways of the desert, its rulers and wild men of seventh century. Muhammad acted the part of a patriot and statesman by combating to such extent as he could the unlimited polygamy of the tribes, their common massacre or burial alive of female children, and the treatment of all women as mere chettels, they could like cattle be seized by the strongest. Their fate as slaves in his day was indeed worse than that of cattle, any polygamy was to them an unspeakable benefit.

He therefore ruled that "men might marry even up to four wifes each, provided they could have and do justly by them." Nor is the result bad, for Muhammadan family life compares favourably with Christian, alike in affection, purity, and peace, and has infinitely fewer divorce cases and scandals.. . It was declared that not even the legal heir for a woman was to succeed to her estate except by her consent, and that as much belief was to be placed on her word as that of the male accuser, even though he were her husband.

### DINET AND SALIMAN

[From "Life of Muhammad the Prophet of Arabia "]

*The Universal Religion.*—Even during Muhammad's life, and in the very beginning, his doctrine asserted its stamp of University. If suitable to all

races, it is equally suitable to all intellects and to
all degrees of civilization. Of supreme simplicity,
as in Mu'taziliticism ; desparately esoteric, as in
Sufiism, bringing guidance and consolation to the
European "Savant"—leaving thought absolutely
free and untrammelled—as well as to the negro of
the Soudan, thereby delivered from the superstition
of his fetishism. It exalts the soul of practical
English merchant for whom " time is money," quite
as much as of a mystical philosopher's; of a
contemplative Oriental ; or of a man of the West
loving art and poetry.

It will even allure a modern medical man, by
the logic of its repeated ablutions and the rhythm of
its bowing and prostration, just as salutary for the
physical well—being as for the health of the soul
itself.

## ALFRED MARTIN

[ From " The Great Religious Teachers of the East "]

*The Successful Prophet.*—Nor is anything in
religion's history more remarkable than the way in
which Muhammad fitted his transfiguring ideas into
the existing social system of Arabia. To his everlasting credit it must be said that in lifting to a
higher plane of life the communities of his day and
place, he achieved that which neither the Judaism

nor the Christianity of Mediaeval Arabia could accomplish. Nay more, in the fulfilment of that civilizing work Muhammad rendered invaluable service, not only to Arabia but also to the entire world.

## PROFESSOR RAM DEV, B. A.

[ Editor of the Vedic Magazine Lahore ]

It is worng to say that Islam was merely spread with sword. It is an established fact that sword was never raised for the propagation of Islam.

If a religion can be spread with sword then let some one come forward and to do so to-day.

## THE EDITOR SAT UPDESH, LAHORE.

They say that Islam was spread by means of sword but we cannot agree with this view, because whatever is forcibly propagated is speedily lost.

Had the propagation of Islam been through compulsion there would not have been any trace of it to-day. But no it is not so. On the other hand we see that Islam is progressing day by day. Why is it so ? Because the Founder of Islam had spiritual power within him. He was all love for mankind, in him the sacred passions of love and mercy were at work all the time. His righteous thoughts guided him.

## Dr GOKALCHAND, Ph D., BARRISTER-AT-LAW, LAHORE.

When the teachings of the Arabian Prophet infused a new life into the uncivilized Arabs, they became the Teachers of the whole Western world and the banner of learning, conquest and divine help began to fly over Bengal on one side and Spain on the other side.

## Dr MARCUS DODS.

"But is Muhammad in no sense a Prophet? Certainly he had two of the most important characteristics of the prophetic order. He saw truth about God which his fellowmen did not see, and he had an irresistible inward impulse to publish this latter qualification, Muhammad may stand comparsion with the most courageous of the heoric prophets of Israel. For the truth's sake he risked his life, he suffered daily persecutions for years, and eventually banishment, the loss of property, of the good-will of his fellow citizens, and the confidence of his friends —he suffered in short as much as any man can suffer

short of death, which he only escaped by flight and
yet he *unflinchingly* proclaimed his message. No
bride, treat or inducement could silence him.
"Though they array against me the sun on the left,
I cannot renounce my purpose." And it was this
persistency, this belief in his call, to proclaim the
Unity of God which was the making of Islam. Other
men have been monotheists in the midst of idolators,
but no other man has founded a strong and enduring
monotheistic religion. The destination in his case
was his resolution that other men should believe.

"The learned doctor further on in his book,
"Muhammad, Buddah, and Christ," remarks—

" No one, I presume, would deny that to Muhammad's contemporaries his religion was an immense
advance on anything they had previously believed
in. It welded together the disunited tribes, and
listed the nation to the forefront of the important
powers in the world. It effected what Christianity
and Judaism had alike effect—it swept away, once
for ever, idolatry, and established the idea of one
true god. Its influence of Arabia was justly and
pathetically put by the Muslim refugees in Abyssinia, who when required to say why they should
not be sent back to Mecca, gave the following account of their religion and what it had done for them:
*O king, we were plunged in ignorance and barbarism, we
worshipped idols, we ate dead bodies, we committed lewdness*

*disregarded family ties and the duties of neighbourhood hospit-
ality, we knew no law but that of the strong, when God sent
among us a Messenger of whose truthfulness, integrity, and
innocense we were aware, and he called us to the unity of God,
and taught us not to associate any god with Him, he forbade
us the worship of idols, and enjoined upon us to speak the
truth, to be faithful to our trusts, to be merciful and to regard
the rights of others, to love our relatives and to protect the
weak, to flee vice and avoid all evil. He taught to offer
prayers, to give alms, and to fast And because we believed in
him and obeyed him, therefore are we persecuted and driven
from our country to seek thy protection*"

### Rev. STEPHENS SAYS.

"The aim of Muhammad was revived among
his countrymen the Arabs, as Moses revived of
among his countrymen, the Jews, the pure faith
their common forefather Abraham. In this he succeeded to a very great extent. For a confused heap
of idolatrous superstitions he substituted a pure
monotheistic faith; he abolished some of the most
vicious pratices of his countrymen, modified others:
he generally raised the moral standard, improved
the social condition of the people, and introduced
a sober and rational cermonial in worship."

"The vices most prevalent inArabia in the time
of Muhammad which are most sternly denounced
and absolutely forbidden in the Quran were drunken

ness, unlimited concubinage and polygamy; the destruction of female infants, reckless gambling superstitious arts of divination and magic. The abolition of some of these evil customs and the mitigation of others, was a great advance in the morality of the Arabs, and is a wonderful and honourable testimony to the zeal and influence of the Reformer. The total suppression of female infanticide and of drunkenness is the most signal triumph of his work."

The reverened gentleman quoted above continues—

"First of all, it must be freely granted that to his own people Muhammad was a great benefactor. He was born in a country where political organizations, and rational faith, and pure morals were unknown. He introduced all three. By a single stroke of masterly genious he simultaneously reformed the political condition, the religious creed, and the moral practice of his countrymen. In the place of many independent tribes he left a nation: for a superstitious belief in gods many and lords many he established a reasonable belief in one Almighty yet Beneficient Beings; taught men to live under an abiding sense of this Being's superintending care, to look to Him as the Rewarder, and to fear him as the Punisher of evil-doers. He vigorously attacked, and modified and suppressed many gross and revolting customs which had prevailed in Arabia down to his time. For an abandoned profigacy was substituted a carefully regulated polygamy, and the practice of destroying female infants was effectually abolished."

" As Islam gradually extended its conquest beyond the boundaries of Arabia, many barbarous race whom it absorbed became in like manner participators in its benefits. The Turk, the Indian, the Negro, and the Moor were compelled to cast away their idols, to abandon their licentious rites and customs, to turn to the worship of one god, to a decent ceremonial and an orderly way of life. The faith even of the more enlightened Persians was purified· he taught that good and evil are not co-ordinate powers, but that just and unjust are alike under the sway of one All-wise Ruler, who ordereth all things in heaven and earth."

" For barbarous nations, then, especially—nations which were more or less in the condition of Arabia itself at the time of Mohammad—nations in the condition of Africa at the present day with little or no civilisation, and without a reasonable religion—Islam certainly comes as a blessing as a turning from darkness to light and from the power of Satan unto God."

## CHAMBER'S CYCLOPEDIA Vol. VI.

"That part of Islam $*$ $*$ $*$ which most distinctly reveals the minds of its author is also its most complete and its most shining part—We mean the ethics to the Quran. They are not found, any more than the other laws, broughtg toether in one, or two, or three Surats but "like golden threads," they are woven into the huge fabric of the religious constitution of Muhammad. Injustice, falsehood. pride, revengefulness, calumny, mockery avarice, prodigality, debauchery, mistrust and suspicion are inveighed against as ungodly and wicked; while benevolence, liberality, modesty, forbearance, and patience, and endurance, frugality, straight forwardness, decency, love of peace and truth, and above all, trusting in one God and' submitting to His will, are considered as the pillars of true piety, and the principle signs of a true believer."

## THE HERBERT LECTURES.

"The law of Islam contains admirable moral precepts, and, what is more, succeeds in bringing them into practice and powerfully supporting their observation."

119

## EDWARD ARNOLD.

The soul of Islam is its declaration of the Unity of god, its heart is the inculcation of an absolute resignation to His will.

## AMEENA AGNES DEAVES.

Islam is a beautiful religion and those who keep the precepts must be living as near to God as it is possible for mankind to do and thereby find peace.

## M. S. BABOONA.

Christianity is commercialism. It says, God must have His pound of flesh and then forgive. Islam is Universalism. It says, God's love knows no measure, on metre. It is unqualified, unbounded, wide as the wide world.

## AHMAD J. MICHEAL.

Now that I have studied the religion (Islam) make bold to say that Islam is the religion after which I was so long hankering, and which thanks Lord, I have at last found to my great consolation and peace of mind. For what is Islam after all but

*Peace*—Peace with God and men, with the Creator as well as His ceratures.

### JAMES A. SPRONLE.

Islam teaches the Unity of God. Other religions have taught the same, but not so emphatically and persistently as in simple confession of the followers of Muhammad.

### PIERRE CRABITES,

Muhammad, thirteen hundred years ago assured to the mothers, wives and daughters of Islam a rank and dignity not yet generally assured to women by the laws of the West.

### REV. MURRY T. TITUS

Islamic brotherhood is a social and spritual fact. Islam is not only a faith, it is a legal system and a social system as well. Islam does possess a brotherhood which is a unifying factor amid the clashes of colour, race, nationality and class. Islamic fraternity is a constan challenge to Christians.

## THE POPULAR ENCYCLOPEDIA (Division)
## VII p 326.

'The language of the Quran is considered the purest Arabic, and contains such charms of style and poetic beauties, that it remains inimitable.' Its moral precepts are pure. A man who should observe them strictly would lead a virtuous life.

### DEAN STANELY, (Eastern Church,) p. 279.

'Within a confined circle the code of the Quran makes doutless a deeper impressions than has been made on Christianity by the code of the Bible.'

### W. IRVING, (Muhammad, p. 208.)

'The Quran contains pure, elevated and benignant precepts.'

### Rev PROFESSOR ROBERTSON.

"It (the Quran) is most unsparing in its condemnation of envy, hypocrisy, hatred, pride, vain glory, un-charitable judgements, and such like, and as emphatic in insisting on the virtues of patience, gratitude, sincerity, and the fear of God."

ENCYCLOPEDIA BRITANNICA Vol. XVI p. 599.

'The contents of the different parts of the Quran are extremely ' varied. Many passages consist of theological and moral reflection. We are reminded of the greatness, the goodness, the righteousness of God, as manifested in nature, in history, and in revelations through the prophets especially through Muhammad. God is magnified as the one, the All-powerful. Idolatry, and all deification of created beings, such as the Worship of Christ, as the son of God, are unsparingly condemned."

Rev. G. MARGOLIOUTH.

" The Koran admittedly occupies an important position among the great religous books of the world. Though the youngest of the epoch-making works belonging to this class of literature, it yields to hardly any in the wonderful effect which it has produce on large masses of men. It has created an all but new phase of human thought, and a fresh type of character."

" Research has shown that what European scholars knew of Greek philosphy, of Mahtematics, of astronomy, and like sciences, for several centuries before the Renaissance, was roughly speaking, all

derived from Latin Treatises ultimately based on
Arabic orginals; and it was the Koran which, though
indirectly, gave the first impetus to these studies
among the Arabs and their Allies. Linguistic
investigations, poetry, ' and other branches of
literature, also make their appearance soon after, or
simultaneously, with the publication of the Koran,
and the literary movement thus initiated has
resulted in some of the finest products of genius and
learning."

*The wonderful reforms effected and extraordinary successes
achieved, by Islam are not only the events of the past but it is
doing the same now in Africa*

### MUNGO PARK.

"The beverages for the pagan Negroe's are beer
and *mead*, of which they frequently drink in excess.
The Muhammadan converts drink nothing but
water."

### Rev. EDWARD BLYDEN.

"If there Christians who are so unmeasured in
their *denunciation* of Muhammadanism could travel
as I have travelled, through those coutries in the
interior of West Africa, and witness, as I have
witnessed the vast contrast between the Pagan and

Muhammadan communities, the habitual listlessness and continued deterioration ot the one, and activity and growth physical and mental, of the other; the capricious and unsettled administration of law, or rather absence of law, in the one, and the tendency to order and regularity in the others; the increasing prevalence of ardent spirits in the one, and the rigid sobriety and *conservative abstemiousness* of the other— they would cease to regard the Mussalman system as an unmitigated evil in the interior Africa."

## LAWTON.

As a religion the Muhammedan religion, it must be confessed, is more suited to Africa than is the Christian religion; indeed, I would even, say that it is more suited to the world as a whole ........

The achievement of the Moslem faith enjoys, I maintain, a definite superiority, in proof of which may be cited Moslem abstinence, sense of fraternity condemnation of usury, and recognition of prophets other than its own. Its quality may be summed up by saying that it takes man as he is, and, while it does not pretend to make a good out of him, seeks to regulate his conduct so that at least he shall become a good neighbour.

## MISS HALIMA MURGURETE LEE.

I cannot understand why Islam should be misrepresented as a belief full of superstition by a class of Protestant and Catholic Ministers and their congregations, when they themselves are bound and fettered in creed and dogma and forms and ceremonies which remind me more of pagan Egypt three thousand years ago than of the twentieth century. I consider myself very fortunate in having found something so much more reasonable.

## SIR CHARLES EDWARD ARCHIBALD -HAMILTON.

There is no religion that is so maligned by the ignorant and biased as is Islam, yet if people only knew it is the only true solution for the problem of socialism, inasmuch as it is the religion of he Strong for the Weak, the Rich for the Poor......

Islam teaches the inherent sinlessness of man. It teaches that man and women came from the same essence, possess the same soul, and have been equipped with equal capablities for intellectual, spiritual and moral attainments.

Ido not think I need say much about the Universal Brotherhood of man in Islam. It is a recognised fact.

## Rev. LACY O'LEARY, D. D.

Declares to the world, to the Christian world especially:—"History makes it clear, however, that the legends of fanatical Muslims sweeping through the world and forcing Islam at the point of the sword upon the conquered races, is one of the most fantastically absurd myths that historians have ever repeated."

## GIBON.

"A pernicious tenet has been imputed to the Muhammadans, the duty of extirpating all other religions by the sword. This charge of ignorance and bigotry is refuted by the Quran, by the history of the Mussalman conquerors, and by their pnblic and legal toleration of the Christian worship."

"The greatest success of his (Muhammad's,) life had been effected by sheer moral force without a stroke of sword."

## Dr. KHALID BANNING.

"At the time of the British occupation of India the Muslims constituted but a tenth of the entire population, whereas tcday they constitute a good fifth—facts which discredited the statement that Islam has been propagated by the sword."

### ANDREW CRICHTON, LL. D.

Their (the Muslims') Schools and academies were the shrines at which the barbarized nations of the West re-kindled the torch of Science and Philosophy.

In the Colleges of Cordova, Siville, France, Germany and England drank from the copious fountain of Arabian literature. In short, without exaggerating the labours of the Arabs, it may be said that we are indebted to them, not only for the revival of the exact and physical sciences, but for most of those useful Arts and inventions that have brought so total a change and given so beneficial and impulse to the literature and civilization of Europe.

———:o:———

# CHAPTER V.

## The Institution of Haj or Pilgrimage.

Haj or holy pilgrimage to Mecca is one of the most prominent duties binding upon muslims. The words of Holy Quran in this respect are plain and emphatic in the following verses :—

"The pilgrimage is in the known months ; then he who proposes there in pilgrimage, let him not be filthy or wicked, or quarrel on the pilgrimage ; and what ye do of good Allah knows it ; and make provisions. but verily, the best provision is piety, and fear Me, O ye who have hearts.

It is no crime to you that ye seek grace from your Lord ; and when ye pour forth from *Arafat*, remember Allah near the Sacred Monument, and remember Him, for that He has guided you when ye were before this certainly of those who go astray.

Then pour ye forth from whence men do pour forth, and ask pardon of Allah; verily, Allah is Forgiving, Merciful.

And when ye have finished your rites ; remember Allah as ye remember your fathers, or with a greater remembrance. And of men is one who

says, Our Lord, give us in this world good; but
there is not for him in the Hereafter any portion.

And of them is one who says, Our Lord, give
us in this world good, and in the Hereafter good,
and save from the torment of the Fire.

These, for them is a portion of what they have
earned; and Allah is swift to reckon. II: 193
to 198.

Verily, the first House of worship founded for
men was surely that at *Makkah* for a blessing and a
guidance to the worlds.

In it are evidences, the standing-place of
Abraham, and whoso enters it is safe. And to Allah
is due from men a pilgrimage to the House, for
whoso can find to it a way. And whoso disbelieves
verily Allah is independent of the worlds.
                                    III: 90, 91, 92.

O ye who believe, kill no game while ye are
on pilgrimage; and whoso kills it among you
purposely, then the compensation is the like of what
he has killed, in cattle two equitable persons shall
judge it among you as an offering to be brought to
the *Ka'bah*, or as an expiation the feeding of the
poor, or an equivalent thereof a fasting, that he
may taste the consequence of his deed. Allah

forgives what is past, and whoso returns, Allah will take vengeance of him; and Allah is Mighty Avenging.

Lawful to you is the game of the sea and to eat thereof as a provision for you and for travellers, but it is unlawful for you to hunt to whom ye shall be gathered.

Allah has made the *Ka'bah* the Sacred House to be a station for men, and the sacred month and the offering and the neck garlands.          V : 96, 97, 98.

And proclaim amongst men the Pilgrimage ; let them come to thee on foot and every fleet camel, arriving from every deep defile.          XXII: 28.

And whoso respects the rites of Allah; verily they are from the piety of hearts. For you therein are advantages until an appointed term then their place of sacrific is at ancient House. And your God is one God ; then to Him be ye Muslims.
XXII: 33, 34, 35.

And the bulky brutes, We have made them for you as symbols of Allah; for you therein is good ; so remember the name of Allah over them as they stand in order; and when they fall down on their sides then eat of them, and feed the contented and those who ask; thus have We pressed them into service for you, that ye may give thanks.

By no means will their meat reach to Allah, nor
their blood but the piety from you alone will reach
to Him ; thus has He pressed them into service for
you, that ye may magnify Allah for that He has
guided you ; and give glad tidings to those who do
good."                                        XXII : 37, 38.

Mecca is the concentric metropolis for perfor
mance of this sacred duty. It is 65 miles from
Jiddah, a port of the Red Sea. In this city
lies that memorable Kaaba which was built long
ago by two revered prophets, Ibrahim and his son
Ismail. Eversince it was held with much esteem
by the people of Arabia. Annual tribal exodus
marked the annals of the Arabian history. Change
of environment inter-mingled with indiscriminate
ideas of the various pilgrims from far and wide,
resulted in the gradual pollution of the Holy place
by the introduction of 360 idols which were later
on destroyed by the Holy Prophet once for all. A
grand mosque now stands there defying the
dogmatic supremacy of idol worship.

This duty of Haj was ordained in the 9th
Muslim era known as Hijree. It should be made
at least once in one's life time by every muslim
provided he is physically fit, of full age, possesses
sufficient money for his journey and for the up-keep
and sustenance of his dependents at home till his
return and that his way to the Holy place is free

from enemies. In the case of a women that lives at
least at 3 days journey from the Holy place, her husband or some one of her near relatives should follow
her. The month specified for undertaking the
pilgrimage is Zul-Hajja but the preparations can
be started well in ahead in the preceding month i. e.
Shawwal and Zulqada.

The "Furz" or obligatory duties of a Hajee
(pilgrim) are three:

1.  To wear "Ihram," consisting of two
    white wrappers; one to be fastened
    round the body and the other thrown
    over the shoulders.

2.  To stand in the plain of "Arafat."

3.  To make the " Tawaf " or circuit round
    the " Kaaba " seven times on the 10th
    Zul Hajj which is called " Tawaf
    Ziarat".

The Waji or important functions are (1) to
stay in "Muzdalfa" on the 9th Zul Hajj after sunset,
(2) to run and partly walk seven times between
Mounts "Safa" and "Marwa", (3) The pilgrims who
are not the residents of "Mecca" should make
another Tawaf or circuit called Tawaf Sadr or
Farewell circuit, (4) to shave the head on the 10th

of Zul-Hujj followed by animal sacrific, (5) Ramil Janar i. e. to throw seven stones in the valley of "Mina."

Nearly five or six miles from Mecca on different sides there are stages called "Miqat". These are Zul Halifoh on the vicinity of Madına-Hujfah on the Syrian road, Qarn on the Najd road, Zate Iraq on the Iraq road, and Yalmalam on the Yalmalam road. When a Hajee reaches any one of these stages he wears his "Ihram." or white wrappers after which he is not allowed to wear any garment such as shirt, trousers, cap etc. He should cover his head and face nor should he cut the hair on the head and the beard. He should abstain from hunting and quarrelling with any one. He must put a stop to sexual intercourse also. Thus consecrated entirely to God, he should proceed towards the sacred territory till he arrives at an elevated place or descends a valley or enters the city of Mecca, when he should mutter continuously " Labbiak " meaning ' here I am O God.' On reaching the enclosure of the city he should at first go to the "Musjidul Horam" and standing before Kaaba recite Allahu-Akber. He then, should kiss " Hajri Aswad " or the Black Stone. Afterwards he should fulfil the ritual of Tawaf or circuit around Kaaba seven times. The permanent inhabitents of Mecca should not perform this Tawaf or

circuit. He Should next climb "Safa" and
"Murwa" and run seven times between these two
mountains. While running he must keep his head
erect and move his shoulders. After performing
this duty, he should live in Mecca wearing his
"Ihram" white wrappers. On the seventh Zul-
Hajj the "Imam" or leader recites the "Kutba"
or sermon and explains to the pilgrims, the fundamental functions of the Hajj. On the eighth day
(Youmi Turwith) the Haji goes to "Mina". It is a
village three and half miles from Mecca. Here he
spends his night. This is "Sunnat" duty. On the
ninth Zul-Hajj (the day of Arfa) after the morning
prayer he goes to "Arafat" (a place twelve miles
from Mecca). Here he finds an occasion to hear
from "Imam" or leader the functions of Ramiul-
janar, animal Sacrifice and Tawaf, or circuit or
presentation. Then the midday and the afternoon
prayers are offered, together with one Azam or call
for prayers and Takbirs. After that he should get
close to the mountain (Juble Rahmat) and stand
there. This is called "Waqf" a fundamental part
of the Hajj. The whole of the Arafat is "Mouqaf"
(standing place) except "Batan Arfa." Standing
here, he should constantly say Takbir, Tahlil, Talib
and repeat Durood and pray for his sins. After
sunset he must proceed to Muzdulfa (a village
between Mina and Arafat). Here at the time of
Isha (night prayer) evening and night prayers are

said with one " Azan " or call for prayer, and one
Takbir.   On the tenth day saying his morning
prayer in darkness, he should start for Mina before
the daybreak and standing in "Balan Wadi" throw
seven pebbles on the three pillars called " Jamarat-
ul-Aqba " saying each time   " Allah-O-Akbar "
(God is the Greatest of all). This done, he should offer
the sacrificial animal and shave his head after
which, he can remove his " Ihram " and re-enter
into his usual customary habits excepting sexual
indulgence, that were prohibited at the time of wearing Ihram.   On the 10th, 11th or 12th Zul-Hajj, he
must go to Mecca and make seven circuits around
Kaaba.' This is called the " Tawaf 'Ziarat " one of
the binding duties of the Hajj.  This Tawaf should
be done without (Ramal) moving the shoulders with
head erect and perform Sayi i e. running between
Safa and Marwa, provided that he had performed
ithese functions at the time of Tawaf Quadoom.  He
should then return to Mina and on the 11th and
12th of Zul-Hajj after noontide throw seven pebbles
at each of the pillars.  If he is a resident of Mina
he should repeat this process on the 13th Zul-Hajj
also  This ceremony over, he should proceed to
Mecca and make Tawaf Sadr (Farewell Circuit).
This is wajab duty exempting the residents of Mecca.
After this, he must drink water from the well of
Zam Zam and kiss the " Multazm " a place between
Hajri Aswad and Kaaba and placing his hands on

the covering of the Kaaba, should weep bitterly to
express sincere and heart-felt regret for having
come to the verge of leaving such a Holy place as
" Musjid Haram ". With this all the functions of
the Hajj terminate.

The duty of Hajj is allied with numerous
benefits, spiritual social and commercial. It is the
best demonstration of a Muslim's love for his God.
He travels thousands of miles from his country,
undergoes every species of trouble, leaves off his
fine garments, clean shaves, sexual pleasures and
other carnal desires, strictly confiding himself to
the duties of Hajj on the wide spread sandy desert
with nothing to befriend him excepting the hot sun
of Arabia scorching him bitterly—all these he does
not for fear or favour of the kings, but just to
please his Creator. He kisses the black stone, not a
sign of worship but the act is the fulfilment of a
commandment ordained as a *token* of profound
respect for that revered prophet Ibrahim who laid it
over there, just as Kalifa Omer once declared
that it was nothing but a lifeless stone and he kissed
it simply because that he saw the prophet doing so.
The Haji makes the Tawaf round the Kaaba and at
the time of prayer turns his face towards it not
because that his God is confined to that small
cavity of brick and mud but merely to obey and
perform the formalities of the commandments of his

Lord. As it is quite necessary for every muslim while reciting his prayer in a congregation to turn his face in one particular direction, and as Kaaba is the most ancient and sacred house it remind us of those pious prophets Ibrahim and Ismail who built it by the order of God. He offers animal sacrifice to perpetuate the memory of that great soul Abraham the father of the faithful who was required by God to sacrifice his son and the way how that worthy son of a worthy father willingly surrendered himself. The merciful God, presented a goat in his place and thus demonstrated His abundance of mercy by saving him from death. Therefore every muslim commemmorates this incident as a typical example of human submission to the will of God. Hajj does not show muslims devotion towards their God, and then stop, but a wonderful revelation of love, equality, fraternity and Universal brotherhood. Prince and peasant, master and slave, abyssinian or a European, white or the black—all stand on one common level and leaving off their racial or social animosities, sink their inferior selves in that ocean of the glory of God.

Notwithstanding the spiritual sphere of amelioration, there are also commercial benefits by means of which the people of Mecca and its vicinity secure a better livelihood, for, the nature is so unfavourable to them that they could scarcely obtain a lucrative job nor reap a good harvest for their maintenance as Arabia is a barren desert. In this manner the Hajj satisfies the proper grouth of the trinity, body, mind and soul.

# CHAPTER VI.
## The ordinance of Ramzan or Fasting.

Fasting claims a particular month in the year among muslims and that month is named after Ramzan which means fasting. It is a " Farz " (obligatory) of every believer to observe the fast during this particular month which comprises 29 or 30 days from one new moon to the other according to the lunar constellation. This was ordained in Madina eighteen months after the Prophet's ' Hijrat ' i. e. flight or retreat from Mecca to Madina. In this connection the Holy Quran inculcates the following :—

"O ye who believe prescribed to you is the fast as it was prescribed to those before you that ye may become pious.

A certain number of days :—But he amongst you who is sick or on a journey, a number of other days ; and upon those who are able is the expiation of feeding a poor man, but whoso is inclined to do a good work—then it is better for him ; but that ye should fast is better for you, if ye only know.

The month of Ramzan, wherein was sent down the Quran for a guidance to men for evidences of guidance, and a distinction. So he amongst you who beholds this month, let him fast it, but he who is sick or on a journey, a number of other days. Allah desires for you ease, and desires not for you difficulty, that ye may complete the number and magnify Allah, for that He has guided you and that ye may give thanks.               II : 179 to 181.

Made lawful for you on the night of the fast is commerce with your wives, they are garment to you and ye are a garment to them. Allah knows that ye defraud yourselves, so He turns to you and excuses you. So now go into them and seek what Allah has prescribed for you, and eat and drink, until a white thread is clearly shown to you from a black thread by the day-break. Then fulfil the fast until the night, and go not into them, but be at your devotions in the places of worship. These are the bounds of Allah; so draw not near thereto. Thus Allah makes His signs clear to men that these may fear to do evil.               II : 189.

Verily, We have revealed it on the Night of Power. And what shall make thee know what the Night of power is? The Night of Power is better than a thousand months. Therein descend the angels and spirit by the permission of their Lord for every matter.

Peace it is until breaking of the dawn!
                          XCVII : 1 to 5.

## TRADITIONS.

The Holy Prophet Mahommad peace and blessings of Allah be on him says:—

Illumine your hearts by hunger, and strive to conquer yourself by hunger and thirst, continue to knock at the gates of Paradise by hunger.

Backbiting vitiates ablution and fasting.

A man whilst fasting must abstain from all bad expressions and not even resent an injury.

A keeper of fast, who doth not abandon lying and detraction, Allah careth not about his leaving off eating and drinking, ( that is, Allah doth not accept his fasting. )

Keep fast and eat also, stay awake at night and sleep also, for verily there is a duty on you to your body, not to labour over much, so that ye may not get ill and destory yourselves ; and verily there is a duty on you to your eyes, ye must sometimes sleep and give them rest ; and verily there is a duty on you to your wife and to your visitors and guests that come to see you ; ye must talk to them, and nobody hath kept fast who fasted always ; the fast of three days in every month is equal to constant fasting ; then keep three days' fast in every month.

Such instances are not few. Moses according to the Holy Bible, observed fast for 40 days. Jews strictly observed fast on the tenth day of thier seventh month as an atonement of their sins. New Testament describes the pathetic narration of Jesus' 40 days fast and the allied spiritual strength he acquired in consequence. From this it could be safely surmised that fasting is not an abrupt outburst of rituals of Islamic zealous expansion and thirst for truth, but a traditional age-long ceremony which has the sanction of the priest and the physician at its back. However, it must not be mistaken that the conditions obtaining in the observance of fast by Jews and Christians are analogous with those of the Muslims. According to the Islam, muslims are required to fast during the Ramzan from sunrise to sunset and abstain entirely all varieties of drinks and eatables and every heinous habit and cohabitation too. It is not all, they should not allow even the least desire for such anxieties to besmear their pure hearts. In fact, they should physically, mentally and spiritually merge away in the feast of the everlasting life and forget entirely all about the world.

Every muslim as soon as he observes the new moon should set about the fast. Young children and lunatics are exempted from it. Travellers, sick persons, mothers with suckling children are free from this obligation. Women in menstruation may postpone the function to a suitable time from when they could continue the fast unhamperred. Of course, this fast has another name called "Qaza" fast. Those who, through infirmity and old age are quite unfit to keep fast should feed a poor person daily. The fast loses all its validity if food is taken by compulsion, medicine is administered even into nose, ears, or a wound in the head, enema is used, food is vomitted, even a drop of water gets into throat while washing the mouth, a meal is taken under mistaken conception that it is night when it is actually a day and the fast is broken on the supposition that the sun has set. In all such cases a "Qaza" fast should be observed in lien of the broken fast to indemnify it. But if the fast is broken deliberately, he must as an atonement for his sin, set free a slave or as alternatives, should either fast continuously every day for two month or should feed sixty persons. The fast need not be considered to have been broken if food or drinks are taken unawares, by kissing a person by applying oil to the beard and antimony to the eyes, by tasting anything under some unavoidable and pressing compulsion. But it anything is tasted without any reason, the fast though not broken, loses all its sanctity. The distinctive feature of a muslim fast is that it is based on moderate principles; neither extremely severe as that of Jews and Christians

who keep it for twenty four hours continuously,
nor so indiscriminate as that of the Hindus who
have quite a good margin of concession for taking
fruits, water or milk during fasting hours. "Sahri"
(a meal taken before sunrise) is a sunnat act.
According to the trabition, it is a blessing and
makes a clear demarkation between the fast
observed by muslims and the others. Some are under
false comprehension that this fast weakens the
system and destroys our constitution. Medical research and our personal experience hold a repugn-
ant view against this pungent idea. By means
of fast every person (excluding very aged
people and tender children and such who are
exempted from the fast) feels rejuvenated and
reinvigorated. The putrial matter of his stomach is
removed gradually and all his internal organs
assume a systematic working order. Such a person
is safe from all those diseases which are the results
of gluttony.

Along with these benefits, it has its spiritual,
social and moral gifts also. It tends to subject the
spirit of man to that of God. It enables the attributes of God to reflect in his soul. Just as God is
free from all passions, so man also for a short time
breaks the bonds of his bodily desires. It humi-
liates the pride of man. Through his sufferings he
begins to feel the suffering of the needy and poor
and sympathises with them. Thus gradually the

145

divine attributes manifested in man move forward
to fill up the gap that separates the higher community from the lower. Besides this, it endows
man with other moral gifts such as patience,
perseverence, contentment etc. Some people consider
that muslim fast is mere abstinance from food, drink
and cohabitation, but it is a mystified notion
altogether. A muslim during his fasting hours
controls all his passions. He avoids every chance
of moral degeneracy such as lying, abusing, back
biting and the such like. There is a tradition
quoted by Abu Hurara according to which the
prophet is reported to have said " Whoever keeps
fast and doesnt give up false speaking and immoral
action, his fast will be of no value, for God is not in
need of his leaving off food or drink ".

Fast is confined to the day, but devotion is not
in conformity to the fast; it extends to full 24
hours. Every night after the "Farz" prayer of
"Isha" he should recite twenty rakats. This is
called "Salatu Tarawih." It is a sunnat obligation. During the prophet's mortal life, it was
recited individually, but later on Kalipha Omar
made congregational recitation obligatory and said
that it was a good Bidat (new order). It is better
to recite at least once during the 30 days of fast,
the whole of Quran in this "Tarwih prayer". Thus
Quran is recited from beginning to end, by millions

of people all over the world during this month—a glorious supplication to the Lord of the Universes.

Another function connected with the Ramzan is "Itakaf". "This is sunnat Muwakkadu". The man who makes " Itakaf" should remain in the mosque during the last ten days of Ramzan. In these days he should entirely devote himself to God. He should not go out of the mosque except for most pressing needs He should spend a greater part of the day and night in reciting Quran and Aurad, meditation and other religious deeds.

Thus a muslim fast when observed properly with all its requirements, tends to obliterate all human drawbacks elevating him to a higher spiritual stage, when he occupies a spiritual sphere of life and justly deserves to be called a " Kalipha " Gods representative on earth. On the completion of 30 days i. e. on the 1st of Shawwal the muslims celebrate the feast known as " Edul-Fiker " more enthusiastically for coming out victoriously out of the trying days of fasting. On this day they wear new clothing, feed the poor and distribute the " Zakat " or poor tax and all the people in the town or City gather together in a Central place and Pray to the Almighty God in open air.

# CHAPTER VII.

## Miraj the Ascension of the Prophet.

———

The question of the actual time of prophet's ascension, presents a bristling controversy as traditionalists are at variance on the point  I do not take cudgels. nor do I assume the role of a critic. It is but certain that the incident had taken place after his ascension.

Accustomed as the prophet is to keep company with young folk, he was one night sleeping in an open space called Hateem beyond the wall of Kaaba.  Jebrail arrived there along with some other angels and conducted him to the well " Zam Zam ". There, laying bare his breast, washed it with the water from " Zam Zam ".  A golden dish was then presented containing religion and wisdom to its brimful.  The angels emitted its contents into his blessed heart and put it back in its place.  Thereupon a wild animal made its appearance.  It was long and white, smaller than a mule and larger than a donkey.  It was called " Buraq ".  The prophet mounted him, and marched on to Jerusalem where the Buraq was tethered to the ring of a door. He, then entered the mosque, and said two  prayer-flexions. There he was offered two vessels; one containing milk and the other wine. The apostle of God dexterously took the milk vessel, which was applauded by Jebrail who said "Had you selected the wine, your followers would have followed an erroneous path". From there he was conveyed to the heaven. He knocked at the door of the first heaven. "Who comes there" came the reply from the Gate Keeper. "It is I" said Jebrail "the Angel of God". Again came the question "Who follows thee?" He said "Mohomed". Gate keeper again queried " Has he been called?" and receiving a reply in the affirmative, the angel opened the door and extended a cordial welcome. There in the first heaven Mohammud perseived a man of full size, on whose left and right sides myriods of shadows remained. When he turned his face towards his right, happiness glistened over his face, but grief and anxiety crowned his brow when he saw towards his left. This venerable soul, while passing the prophet exclaimed "Welcome pious son, O, pious prophet". Mohummed was perplexed to see this curious figure and asked the angel to put him on the know of the affair. "Hear" said Jebrail "this is my father Adam, the first man on the earth, the shadows on his right and left are the souls of his good and bad sons respectively. His feelings assume happiness and grief in accordance

to the virtue and vice clinging on his sides." He
then proceeded to the second heaven where he
beheld Isa (Jesus) and Yahya (John the Baptist).
They both felicitated him with cordial invitation.
In the third heaven, he met Yusuf (Joseph), in the
fourth, Idris (Enock) and in the fifth Haroon
(Aaron). At every stage he met with a warm
reception and cordial greetings were showered on
him. In the sixth heaven he saw Musa (Moses)
who welcomed him but began to weep while
Muhammad conducted his steps further on. An
unknown solemn voice asked " Why dost thou
weep?" " Yes, I weep " replied Moses "for can't
you see that a youth has received a mission after
me ; and that youth will find followers who could
enter paradise more advantageously than myself?".
In this celestial perambulation, he reached the 7th
heaven where he saw Ibrahim who with overwhelming happiness exclaimed " Come along pious
Prophet, Welcome unto thee pious son" Jebrail at
once told Muhammad that the speaker was Abrahm
his ancestor, the father of the faithful. The revelation of Ibrahim's vision was a glorious one. He
was leaning against "Baitul Mamur", the heavenly
tabernacle which is a resort of seventy thousands of
angels everyday, the happiest place. Once they
get in they cannot return again. Now came
Muhammad to the garden of paradise which he
surveyed in detail. This done, Jebrail took him to

"Sidratulmuntah" (the Lote tree which marks the boundary). The tree was resplendent with fascinating brilliance. After passing the tree, Jebrail, tarried behind and said "I can no more go further. This is my limit. One more step, I am burnt to ashes". The prophet with one pathetic look at the angel and a steadfast sight towards his pursuit walked all alone beyond many curtains and arrived at the foot of "Arsh" (the great throne) where encouraging sound "Approach nearer" was heard at short intervals. Approaching nearer, he saluted the Lord of the Universe in the following befitting words. They are simple and forceful devoid of superfluous phraseology. Mark how he said. "Humble salutations and righteous greetings unto God". "Salutation to thee O, Prophet and the mercy of God and his blessings on thee" came the reply. The prophet ejaculated ' Salutation to us and to the pious servants of God". Whereupon the angels replied with profound respect "We testify that there is no God but Allah and Muhammad is the apostle and servant of God". A mysterious conversation ensued between the God and his apostle, which baffles human philosophy. Words cannot explain its veracity and immagination cannot fathom its depth. The wonderful spectacle of God of Universes talking to his selected prophet in the uppermost strata of heavens is presented here.

Awe-inspiring is the scene, bewildering is its significance and mysticism envelops the incident for
human thought is moribund to the sharp touch of
this sensitive revelation Wounderful gifts were
offered to the prophet as a result of the talk. They
are 1, the last verses of Sura Baqr which deal with
the fundamental principles of Islam, 2, he received
devine promise that all his followers would be
pardoned except those who committed " shirk ", 3,
fifty prayer-flexions became obligatory during one
day and night.

The Prophet during his descension, encountered
with Musa, who asked " How many prayers are
imposed upon thy followers." " Fifty prayers each
day and night " said the prophet. Musa exclaimed
" I have tested the children of Israil. Your people
are too feeble to execute fifty rounds of prayers. I
requested God to reduce the number to five," and
thus Musa asked Muhammud to go back to God and
obtain a reduction in the number. However the
prophet expressed his inability to do that on the
plea that it was a shameful entreaty. The Prophet
returned from heaven to Jerusalem and there he
beheld a group of prophets. Moses and Ibrahim
were in brisk prayers. Refreshed with the heavenly
solicitude, the Holy Prophet arose from his bed with
lively vigour and expouned all his miraculous
experiences in his heavenly sojourns to his people.

But, the infedels, put a deaf ear and accused him of falsehood. His opponents challenged him to give information about the farther temple. The prophet was at first confused, but soon the temple was just before his eyes and he gave keen replies to their astonishment.

There has been much controversy among Ulmas whether this ascension was bodily or spiritual or during his sleep or before. Majority of the Ulmas beleive it to be a bodily one and that he was not succumbed to the oblivion of sleep during his ascension, on the following grounds :—

Quran has mentioned the notable event in the 17th Sura as follows: "Praise be to him who carried his servant (Abd) by night from "Musjid Haram" to "Musjid Aqsa". The word Abd (servant) implies body and soul, so what objection to doubt that he was bodily lifted up. If it had been a spiritual ascension, there was no occasion for the infedels to be surprised. As soon as they heard the description of the journey they began to laugh at the prophet and accused him of falsehood. Had it been a spiritual one or a vision in the dram, it would not have been considered as an impossible incidence. It is already described in the events of ascension that the prophet drank the cup of milk and mounted Buraq. This cannot be achieved

while in a spiritual body and it is not necessary too.
The possibility of the heavenly journey in human
body is refuted now-a-days by many an educated
muslims as being quite irrational and most un-
scientific. Before coming to any definite conclusion
on the matter, they should glance over the spiritual
conquests of the modern age. In the present
century the wonderful achievements of the mes-
merists and hypnotists have baffled the minds of
even the most confirmed materialists Their actions
are of different kinds. Contents of the heart are
disclosed, bodily diseases are eradicated, from a
long distance too, lifeless objects are given
movement, human beings are magnetically drawn
towards another quite unintentionally on the part of
the subjected parties. All such miraculous deeds
are performed by ordinary spiritualists. When
selfish mortals could bewilder the modern world so
much, is it impossible for saints to perform wonders
surpassing those of the materialistic human beings.
Some rationalists think that the bodily ascension is
against the laws of nature that govern the universe
but they are in dark and their knowledge is limited
to a certain limitation. They are like a child that
denies the existance of a comet because it has never
seen it. Ignorance of the existance of a certain
object is no guarantee that it does not exist.
Divine laws are far beyond the human compresen-

sion. According to our belief, miracles are the direct belief, miracles are the direct action of God. Sometimes He, changes his usual course to countenance the glory of his followers. So this ascension of the prophet also is believed to be the result of divine power. According to the Quran, God himself carried his servant from Musjid Haram to Musjid Aqsa. If the subject is tackled through the correct angle of vision, the opponents of this truth will be adquately satisfied.

## SIGNIFICANCE OF ASCENSION.

By this ascension the apostle of God met some of the renowned prophets such as Abraham, Jesus, Moses etc. He had seen all the wonders of the heavens, reached to that eminent place which can never be seen by ordinary mortals or even angels, where a mysterious conversation took place between him and the God of the world. On his return he received many a divine favours. He is the only soul that brought back to the world the revelations of the heavens above and explained to the world as a mortal speaking with people face to face. What a wonderful mission.

# CHAPTER VIII

---

## What is Islam?

---

[ *The following is a very brief account of Islam, and some of its teaching.* ]

SLAM, THE RELIGION OF PEACE.—The word Islam literally means: (1) Peace; (2) the way to achieve peace; (3) submission; as submission to another's will is the safest course to establish peace. The word in its religious sense signifies complete submission to the Will of God.

OBJECT OF THE RELIGION.— Islam provides its followers with the perfect code whereby they may work out what is noble and good in man, and thus maintain peace between man and man.

THE PROPHETS OF ISLAM.—Muhammad, popularly known as the prophet of Islam, was, however, the last Prophet of the Faith. Muslims, i. e. the followers of Islam, accept all such of the world's prophets, including Abraham, Moses and Jesus, as revealed the Will of God for the guidance of humanity.

THE QURAN.—The Gospel of the Muslim is the Quran. Muslims believe in the Divine origin of every other sacred book, but, inasmuch as all such previous revelations have become corrupted through human interpolation, the Quran, the last Book of God, came as a recapitulation of the former Gospels.

ARTICLES OF FAITH IN ISLAM.—These are seven in number · belife in (1) Allah; (2) angels; (3) books from God; (4) messengers from God; (5) the hereafter; (6) the measurement of good and evil, (7) resurrection after death.

The life after death, according to Islamic teaching, is not a new life, but only a continuance of this life, bringing its hidden realities into light. It is a life of unlimited progress; those who qualify themselves in this life for the progress will enter into Paradise, which is another name for the said progressive life after death, and those who get their faculties stunted by their misdeeds in this life will be the denizens of the hell—a life incapable of appreciating heavenly bliss, and of torment—in order to get themselves purged of all impurities and thus to become fit for the life in heaven. State after death is an image of the spiritual state, in this life.

The sixth article of faith has been confused by some with what is popularly known as Fatalism.

A Muslim neither believes in Fatalism nor Predestination; he believes in Premeasurement. Everything created by God is for good in the given use and under the given circumstances. Its abuse is evil and suffering.

PILLARS OF ISLAM.—These are five in number: (1) declaration of faith in the Oneness of God, and in the divine Messengership of Muhammad, (2) prayer; (3) fasting; (4) almsgiving; (5) pilgrimage to the Holy Shrine of Mecca.

ATTRIBUTES OF GOD.—The Muslims worship one God—the Almighty, the All-knowing, the All-just, the Cherisher of all the Worlds, the Friend, the Guide, the Helper. There is none like Him. He has no partner. He is neither begotten nor has He begotten any son or daughter. He is Indivisible in Person. He is the light of the heaven and the earth, the Merciful, the Compassionate, the Glorious, the Magnificent, the Beautiful, the Eternal, the Infinite, the First and the Last.

FAITH AND ACTION.—Faith without action is a dead letter. Faith is of itself insufficient, unless translated into action. A Muslim believes in his own personal accountability for his actions in this life and in the hereafter. Each must bear his own burden, and none can expiate for another's sin.

ETHICS IN ISLAM.—"Imbue yourself with divine attributes." says the noble Prophet. God is the prototype of man, and His attributes from the basis of Muslim ethics. Righteousness in Islam consist in leading a life in complete harmony with the Divine attributes. To act otherwise is sin.

CAPABILITIES OF MAN IN ISLAM.—The Muslim believe in the inherent sinlessness of man's nature which, made of the goodliest fibre' is capable of unlimited progress, setting him above the angels and leading him to the border of Divinity.

THE POSITION OF WOMAN IN ISLAM.—Men and women come from the same essence, posses the same soul, and they have been equipped with equal capability for intellectual, spiritual, and moral attainment. Islam places man and woman under like obligations, the one to the other.

EQUALITY OF MANKIND AND THE BROTHERHOOD OF ISLAM.—Islam is the religion of the Unity of God and the equality of mankind. Lineage, riches and family honours are accidental things; virtue and the service of humanity are the matters of real merit. Distinctions of colour, race and creed are unknown in the ranks of Islam. All mankind is of one family, and Islam has succeeded in welding the black and the white into one fraternal whole.

PERSONAL JUDGMENT.—Islam encourages the exercise of personal judgment and respects difference of opinion, which, according to the sayings of the Prophet Muhammad, is a blessing of God.

KNOWLEDGE.—The pursuit of knowledge is a duty in Islam, and it is the acquisition of knowledge that makes men superior to angels.

SANCTITY OF LABOUR.—Every labour which enables man to live honestly is respected. Idleness is deemed a sin.

CHARITY.—All the faculties of man have been given to him as a trust from God, for the benefit of his fellow-creatures. It is man's duty to live for others, and his charities must be applied without any distinction of person. Charity in Islam brings man nearer to God. Charity and the giving of alms have been made obligatory, and every person who possesses property above a certain limit has to pay a tax, levied on the rich for the benefit of the poor.

PRINTED AT PREMIER PRESS, SECUNDERABAD.

Ingram Content Group UK Ltd.
Milton Keynes UK
UKHW022234190423
420461UK00005B/101

9 781341 736070